The Waves We Ride

A Woman's Journey of Overcoming
Life Adversities and Embracing
Change

Ladyane Lima

Praise for The Waves We Ride

"The Waves We Ride was a compelling read for me, a 33-year Wall Street veteran who also raised a family during that time. Although I wish I had this book 33 years ago when I was starting my Wall Street journey, it has empowered me today to embrace change in my current life and is incredibly timely for me! I wholeheartedly recommend this to young women starting their careers and older veterans, as we are riding waves our whole lives."

Kit Turner, Executive at an Investment Bank

"Ladyane shares her personal journey from a small town in Brazil to the challenges she faced in New York City while pursuing her dreams. She demonstrates what can be achieved by confronting fears and self-doubt head-on. Her story and determination to succeed left me truly inspired."

Deborah Farley, Marketing Professional

"The Waves We Ride offers a perspective on the beauty of recognizing opportunities, even during challenging and turbulent times. It reminded me that life is about taking a deep breath and being open to new dives. I felt deeply moved at several points and connected with moments that made me reflect on my own life."

Juliana Fittipaldi, Fashion Designer NYC

NEWSLETTER SIGN UP

Sign up for bonus content including newsletters on personal growth,
living your best life,
career-related stories and more at
https://www.ladyanelima.com/

Book Cover designed by MiblArt

Edited by Kat Betts of Element Editing Services & Larissa Rinaldi

First edition 2024

ISBN hardcover (979-8-9919423-0-0); ISBN paperback (979-8-9919423-1-7); ISBN ebook (979-8-9919423-2-4)

DEDICATION

To my mom, the one who taught me the meaning of personal growth.
To my sister, the one who showed me the way of many possibilities.
To my husband, the one who gives me the tools to enable my transformation.
And, to my children, the ones who allow me to "be."

CONTENTS

INTRODUCTION

W ELCOME, DEAR FRIEND; I'M so glad you're here, joining me on this journey through *The Waves We Ride - A Woman's Journey of Overcoming Life Adversities and Embracing Change*. As you settle in, imagine us sitting together, perhaps with a comforting cup of tea or a glass of wine, chatting like old friends about life, dreams, and the countless waves we ride in life.

My name is Ladyane, and I'm a Latina woman, an immigrant, and a former Wall Street executive who has journeyed through the challenges and triumphs that life has presented. I've learned that life's adversities often bring us invaluable lessons, and it is through sharing our experiences that we can uplift and empower one another. This book is a heartfelt compilation of my journey, infused with insights, stories, and lessons that I believe will resonate with you.

I decided to write this book because I deeply believe in the power of shared experiences. We all have our own waves to ride—moments of joy, pain, struggle, and triumph. By opening up about my life, I hope to create a space where we can reflect on our experiences together and find inspiration in one another's stories. My journey is just one of many, but I hope it sparks something within you—whether it's the courage to chase a dream, the strength to overcome obstacles or the conviction to embrace the beautiful chaos of life.

As you read, I want you to feel like we are in a safe space where you can take a moment for yourself and reflect on your journey. Let's explore the challenges we face as women, the dreams we nurture, and the power we hold to create change in our lives and the lives of those around us. I hope that through these pages, you will find encouragement and inspiration to take bold steps toward your aspirations and embrace the waves of change.

So, pour yourself that drink, make yourself comfortable, and let's dive into this adventure together. I can't wait to share my stories with you, and I hope they resonate with your own journey, inspiring you to reach for greater heights and embrace the beautiful possibilities ahead.

With warmth and gratitude,

Ladyane.

Chapter 1

WHERE ARE YOU, LADYANE LIMA?

Listen, girl, it is not going to be easy. But it is going to be magical.

S HOULD I STAY, OR should I run? Goodness—none of this crossed my mind when I got up on that stage to deliver my speech on a beautiful evening in May 2012 at the Grand Hyatt New York Hotel. I was ready, but I got nervous. Suddenly, there I was—a young Latina about to graduate from college with honors and enjoying the guarantee of a job at a top international investment bank in New York City.

When I heard my name, "Ladyane Lima," followed by "Where are you?" I looked at my village for emotional support. My sister, my mentor, and my soon-to-be husband were sitting at one of the tables in the middle of the crowd, cheering and applauding like no one else was in the room. I thought I was a rock star.

The Financial Women's Association, commonly known as FWA, invited me to be the student speaker of the 2012 class due to my academic and professional achievements. The dinner followed a cocktail reception where I delivered my speech. Upon making eye contact with my emotional support village, off I went. I decided to stay, walk up to the microphone, and deliver my speech. Suddenly, all I could think of was my speech coach's advice—*You wrote the speech. You got this.*

A flashback goes through my mind as I walk to the stage. Picture this: I am twenty-four years old, born and raised in Brazil; I am about to deliver a speech to more than 400 top executive women from all sorts of ethnicities and backgrounds who, just like me, worked very hard to earn their place in the corporate ladder. I was nervous—you could tell if you watched the speech. But let's get back to the stage, shall we? Despite the pressure I put on myself to deliver a perfect speech (someone said perfectionist?), I felt confident. I felt prepared. I had such joy in my face. I was ready for the spotlight. I was enjoying the young, confident, professional version of Ladyane. I firmly believed I deserved and had earned my spot on that stage. After all, I had worked incredibly hard and put in the effort. As I delivered the speech, I saw the admiration and joy on people's faces, which was incredibly comforting. Afterward, women came up to share how inspiring they found my journey. Their reactions were deeply touching. The speech captures essential aspects of my story, and I'm excited to share it with you here:

"Good evening, ladies and gentlemen and FWA members.

It is an honor to be here tonight with you.

I was born in a very small town in Brazil, called Cuiabá, close to one of the biggest swamps in the world, called Pantanal. In fact, the swamp is actually bigger than the town. Back then most of the streets had no pavement, houses were very modest with brick walls and no paint. This is where I come from, and I want to share my story of necessity, hope, and opportunity with all of you tonight.

My background led me to have the drive to succeed, to have a better life. When I was thirteen years old my family and I moved to Rio de Janeiro looking for greater opportunities. When I was twenty years old I joined my older sister here in New York City to attend college. That was four years ago.

From then on, my life has been a hope-opportunity cycle. My necessity to succeed has driven me to paths that I never envisioned for myself. This same necessity led me to learn more about the Financial Women's Association at Baruch College. And so when I found FWA, I knew I needed to embrace the opportunity.

FWA has given me opportunities that go beyond the scope of any young professional such as myself. I learned discipline, the art of networking, and technical skills. During the breakfasts and luncheons, I had opportunities to expand my professional network and learn different ways to leverage my skills. FWA prepared me to be more competitive, to perform at my full potential at any given task.

My mentor, [Sophia Luthernan], has become my friend. She is not only supportive but challenges me on many levels. Our relationship is very collaborative with constant communication and exchange of ideas. I will always be thankful for the knowledge she has shared with me.

While attending college full time, working part-time, volunteering, and being an active FWA mentee, I was able to spend the summer of last year at [Bank 1] which led to a full time employment opportunity. I am happy to say I will start this June. FWA essentially gave me the path to success, the opportunity for me to take and succeed. I am not only grateful for this but also want to maintain my attachment to FWA in the future.

Today, the skills I have learned and nurtured through the Financial Women's Association gave me the confidence I need in order to launch my career. Thanks to FWA, I am very happy to say that things I want to accomplish come out of options—options and not necessities."

Thank you!"

Life was not as simple as deciding to pursue my college education abroad and getting it done. Life started when I was six years old, and shortly after, everything turned into the opposite of simple.

I only remember a little before that. However, all my childhood experiences and memories inevitably shaped my core belief system. These experiences shape how I think and perceive the world. But not to worry, my friend. In this book, I plan on something other than telling you what a belief system is and what I believe in. That could be boring.

Instead, in this book, I will tell you how a Brazilian girl born in a small town ended up having a stellar academic journey in the US, a reputable professional career of nearly ten years on Wall Street, how she ended up getting married, converting to Judaism, and becoming the mother of the three most precious little human beings in the world. Today, I am motivated and inspired by the drive to make decisions based on options, not necessities — a valuable skill I learned during my time as an FWA mentee.

Hang tight—I do not mean to present facts and my life timeline. I mean to share with you how, in many moments, I felt so overwhelmed and scared that I shut down and cried, but the next day, I would get up and keep going. What I hope by doing this is to motivate you. I hope I can support you in searching and finding yourself amid the obstacles and fears that blindside us. I hope to inspire you to embrace changes.

Let me ask you for a favor before we continue. Picture yourself swimming in the open ocean. Now, picture yourself going through the waves. The waves are the emotions in life. Sometimes, these waves turn into tsunamis. The tsunamis are emotional outbursts—essentially, tsunamis represent that overwhelming feeling that may make you want to run away or shut down. It is when you feel you've lost your ground. We all have waves to ride. We are all faced with changes in life and the emotions that come with them. However, how we navigate challenges and the reasons behind our actions are crucial factors in overcoming life adversities. When you accept the wave, navigate through it, and are clear about your motivation and intention, there is pure joy, confidence, and happiness. In this book, I will share my waves with you, how I rode them, my motivations, and how I transformed because of them—from childhood to today.

Why am I reopening healed wounds and exposing my journey with you? I went through some hardcore shaking moments in the last couple of years since I decided to take a career break to dedicate myself intentionally and emotionally to my family. During this time, I realized that sharing my journey could inspire other women to find their superpowers and nurture their ability to ride their fears, insecurities, achievements, and failures – To ride all the waves in life like I did. I am confident you will find yourself somewhere in my journey and will be able to relate to the experiences I went through. I hope that by being able to relate to these experiences, you will find the strength to embrace positive changes and live your best life.

Writing this book helped me to understand my journey and its purpose entirely. It was challenging to break from nearly a decade of hard work on Wall Street, however, pressing the emotional reset button allowed me to do this, which is something I enjoy—to write. Writing this book enabled me to understand my feelings from childhood to today. Rushing through life sometimes prevents us from profoundly feeling, recognizing, and accepting emotions. Rushing through life sometimes prevents us from healthily riding the emotional waves and changes in life. Writing this book also helped me understand that my current daily responsibilities as a stay-at-home mother do not define who I am, but add to a great set of endless possibilities for my future.

Writing this book helped me comprehend my several transformations to achieve specific life goals. Transformation is beneficial when done in a healthy manner and for the right reasons—reasons you genuinely believe in. I truly hope that sharing some memorable moments of my life and the emotional waves I went through, as well as the lessons I learned, will help you see yourself in some of these moments and brighten up that vision that gets blurred sometimes when we are uncertain of decisions, emotions, and actions.

Here is what I wish today's Ladyane would have told the eighteen-year-old Ladyane, who was about to leave her life behind in Brazil to start brand new in the US:

"Listen, girl, it is not going to be easy. But it is going to be magical. There will be tears. There will be heart-racing moments. There will be uncertainties. There will be doubts (the worst nightmare for a Virgo like yourself). But there will also be you. You will be there; ultimately, you will do what is best for you and try to learn as much as possible. And that's all that there is. There will be tears of joy and tears of sadness. There will be happiness because of love. There will be more tears of joy. There will be happiness for achieving things due to your hard work. For that, don't just wait and see. Initiate (be an initiator) and learn. It will all work out."

Hearing these words of affirmation would have made an enormous difference to me in the days when I wanted to give up and return to Brazil. Or, when I had just given up on interviewing at so many banks when I was in college trying to land a job to stay legally in the US. Or when I wanted to give up on my career, or when I doubted my ability to be a good mom. So, friend, print these words and place them in front of your work computer or your phone screen — Listen, girl, it is not going to be easy. But it's going to be magical. Do whatever you need to remind yourself that everything will work out.

Are you ready to ride this wave with me? Are you ready to embrace personal transformation? Where do you see yourself? Is it in the Latina college student, the Wall Street young professional, the Jewish woman, or the mother of three? Can you see yourself in more than one? Ride the wave with me. Embrace your change. I hope you enjoy it.

Riding the Wave – My Context

I recognize and accept my emotions without judgment. I choose not to suppress them or avoid them. I choose to embrace them. I choose to validate them.

Before I go ahead and share my journey with you, I wanted to take a moment to provide some context about this book's title. At the beginning of my behavioral therapy journey, which started months before I became a mother, I thought I should tackle my ever-increasing anxiety so that I could feel better prepared to welcome my first daughter into the world. Although I started seeing a psychologist in 2014, it wasn't until 2022 that I first heard about the strategy of riding the wave within the Dialectical Behavioral Therapy (DBT) approach. This changed everything for me.

But what is Dialectical Behavioral Therapy? In a nutshell, DBT was created in the 1980s by Doctor Marsha Linehan and combines elements of Cognitive Behavioral Therapy (CBT) with mindfulness practice. Upon further research of my own, I learned that DBT is particularly helpful for individuals who experience emotional traumas. From my experience, applying the "riding the wave" strategy works like this: *I recognize and accept my emotions without judgment. I choose not to suppress them or avoid them. I choose to embrace them. I choose to validate them. And I choose to take as long as needed to go through them because they are real and mine.*

I have become lighter since I learned about the "riding the wave" strategy. I doubt myself much less. I judge less. I accept more. I also use this approach with my children today—I validate their emotions. I help them practice kindness with themselves by using their inner voices to truly understand and accept their feelings. These are essential tools for them to grow up emotionally capable of handling life. Do I know for sure this will work for them? Am I a psychologist? No and no. And look, I am not saying I do not want my children to rely on me for emotional support when they grow up—on the contrary. However, I want them to have one or two tricks up their sleeves when out there and not within my arms. Every day, I can see they appreciate the knowledge and benefit of having their tools to ride an emotional wave. I think I am okay with that for now. Put it this way: I would rather have them practice this muscle than shut the muscle entirely and not enable them to express their emotions. It isn't always easy. When I talk more about "Mama Brasicana" — a Brazilian mother who has left Brazil and moved to the U.S, but shares everything about her original culture and language for the sake of leaving an emotional legacy to her children — I will share some challenges I experienced as a mother of three children under nine, especially during pandemic days. More to come on that. But before I talk more about my children, how about I share some of my childhood with you? Let's go back to the 1990s— to a small town called Cuiabá, Brazil.

Chapter 2

CHILDHOOD

Always trying to blend in and adapt, just like a
chameleon — reacting to the changes rather than
navigating and embracing them.

I WAS BORN IN a small town called Cuiabá, in Mato Grosso, Brazil. Cuiabá is extremely hot and humid. I remember the weather was always good for swimming. Once, a reporter fried an egg on the asphalt just to show how hot it was. Later, I read that for you to fry an egg on the asphalt, the surface temperature must be at least 140 Fahrenheit—can you imagine? But let's get back to my childhood, shall we?

A typical childhood path includes playing and going to school, having fun, and living without concerns or problem-solving responsibilities. Children are not expected to cope with atypical life events on their own, they need the emotional support of a "trust person," usually their parents. Parents form the child's emotional support village, helping them grow up to be confident and calm.

My childhood took an atypical path when I was seven years old. Everything changed. My dad passed away when I was seven years old. His passing happened almost as if in slow motion, which made the entire experience nearly unbearable to a seven-year-old girl. His illness slowly took over, and he eventually surrendered. I saw him very ill and taken over by his illness. This image to a seven-year-old can be traumatizing if a child does not have the proper emotional support to understand it and cope with it. I lacked that very much-needed emotional support. Here, my friend, is where I had my first life challenge. I did not know then. I came to understand it after motherhood. More to come on that. Losing my dad at the age of seven was an emotional wave (more like a tsunami).

When my dad passed, my mother was busy trying to figure things out and provide us with the proper care. His battle with his illness was so traumatizing to me that I ended up missing the equivalent of an entire school year because I feared that he would be gone by the time I returned from school. My seven-year-old brain then concluded that I would prolong his presence with us if I stayed home instead of going to school. Get this: the school bus would pull over at my front door to pick me up, and I would run away from my mom, yelling, "I am not going!" while she chased me through the backyard. My dad used to watch and laugh. My mom used to get furious. I didn't care—I wanted to stay by his side.

I adored my dad. My dad was my hero. My dad taught me how to swim when I was still a baby before I even learned how to walk! As a mother today, I see swimming as a life skill. My dad was able to teach me a life skill before he passed. I am thankful for that.

My dad never measured his efforts to provide us with everything we needed. He offered the best education for as long as he was alive. He gave me lots of love and care. Picture this: a six-year-old girl playing around in the backyard of her house. There was a big swimming pool, playground, and a real-kid-sized dollhouse with real furniture inside. I used to spend a lot of time playing inside my dollhouse. My dad helped me furnish the house – he bought little sofas and chairs, a little toy lamp, and even a toy stove. I loved it! I remember our home was under renovation, so some construction workers and equipment were always lying around. Shortly after we moved into the house, my parents paused the renovation. Unknown to me then, we paused the renovation because we ran low on cash. My parents spent everything on my dad's illness treatment and basic expenses.

Suddenly, my dad would go away for days. He would return sicker than when he left. It was frightening to witness my dad's health deteriorating right before my eyes. I do not remember anyone talking to me about it, nor do I remember asking anyone about what was going on. Witnessing my dad's serious illness was the first wave I remember riding with not much preparation or emotional guidance.

My Dad, The Husband & Riding the Second Wave

My dad, however, had a different side to him. He was not a good husband. You see, my dad had drinking problems. Because of his drinking problems, resentment and sadness would sometimes replace the superhero image I had of him. Take a look at this: You are a child, and you see your dad raising his voice at your mother and attempting to hurt her physically. You run away because you are afraid of what you may see. And then you hear the bangs and loud voices. What would you do? I hid and waited. Again, no one ever came to talk to me about it. Do you see the pattern here? Right, there was no emotional presence from an adult to emotionally guide my little seven-year-old self. And so, the trauma begins.

Let's pause for a moment and go back to my definition of a belief system. The *belief system*, in my view, is essentially the projection of all my experiences in life. For example, say a girl grows up experiencing abandonment from the people she loves the most, the people she is supposed to be deeply connected with. When this girl grows up, she will manifest this abandonment in the relationships she develops, believing abandonment is her fate. She will believe in this because she knows nothing other than this—how could she? It is all she has experienced in life. Anything other than this would be unknown and foreign to her. There you have it then—being abandoned becomes part of her *belief system.*

It wasn't until I was about twenty, when I met "the guy" and fell deeply in love, that I realized my lack of trust in the marriage institution —*Goodness, what now? I do not see myself getting married. He is talking about marriage. What should I do? Do I tell him about my fears? Do I tell him I do not know about marriage any other way?*

So many things were going through my mind. The worst fear: *What if I tell him about all these fears and what I witnessed as a child, and he runs away?* I feared he would disappear, thinking, *This girl has heavy emotional baggage—she means trouble. I'm outta here.* That's when I realized that my emotional experiences and memories of my dad as an abusive husband led me to believe the institution of marriage was broken. For most of my life, I believed there was no such thing as a happy and healthy marriage. So, my initial reaction when I realized I was falling for my husband was to run away because I simply did not believe that marriages worked. I am glad he stuck around and persuaded me. I am glad I did not run away. I am thankful for personal experiences and how they shape our belief systems. I am grateful for riding this second wave — for allowing myself the ability to face my fear but still embrace the opportunity to fall in love and grow a family.

My Dad Passes Away, My Mother Rises Stronger & Riding the Third Wave

Here I am—a seven-year-old girl who just lost her dad. I look and see my mother crying—but her tears were not of sadness. They felt more like tears of desperation mixed with relief. Desperation because when my dad died, he left nothing but bills to pay. We were homeless. Relief because she was finally free—no more abusive husband. No more fighting to get a divorce. She is a real-life example of personal transformation. She was thirty-five years old when my dad died. She had to reinvent herself. A new mother was born. A go-getter. A doer. A fighter. From that moment on, I saw a woman I had never seen before and admired her deeply—a better version of herself. My mom taught me that we can reinvent ourselves and rise stronger despite the obstacles and pain.

Shortly after my dad died, we lived at my godparents' house for a while. I did not take his passing lightly. I used to cry a lot. Every time I would see a picture of my dad shortly after his passing, I would cry. I would ask why he had to die. My mother would come and hug me. No words—just silence. And there I was, again, riding my wave alone. There was no emotional support in the sense of talking about what death means and how we cope with it. There was logistical support of putting food on the table and having a roof over our heads. I scraped my "wave" out of the way for a very long time and tried to keep myself afloat. I did not know how to recognize, define, accept, and manage my emotions. No one ever guided me emotionally through the process.

But you see, not knowing how to recognize, accept, and ride your wave is not sustainable. Sooner or later, you may drown.

When I was about nine years old, my mother managed to buy a little house for us. My mother had two jobs. During weekdays, she would drive all over town selling shirts. During the weekends, she would quickly visit Paraguay to buy imported goods and sell them at discounted prices back in Brazil. She needed to do this to be able to pay the monthly bills. Experiences shape our belief systems. Seeing my mother working so hard made me believe in two things—If I work hard, I can be financially stable. If I work hard, I can have financial independence.

My mother's plan did not work for too long. There was no perspective of a better future for us had we stayed in Cuiabá. My mother was barely making it through the bills. She had family in the big cities—Sao Paulo and Rio de Janeiro. So off we went. When I was ten, we moved to Sao Paulo. It wasn't easy. Sao Paulo was chaotic and immense—it frightened me. But we were in pursuit of a "better future."

What does a "better future" mean? For us back then, it meant having more educational, financial, and cultural options. Having a "better future" meant not being limited to only a handful of options. If we stayed in Cuiabá, we would probably (and unfortunately) have limited access to education, impacting everything else in our lives. I did not know all of this back then; how could I? I was a child. However, I can tell you that from a very early age, I knew I did not want financial instability. Seeing my mother count money and choosing which bills to pay was not so reassuring. But I was still a child—it did not impact me as much.

I was always so scared and felt lonely in Sao Paulo. I was the first to leave the house early in the morning. My school was far from home, so I was the first stop on the school bus. I would ride about thirty to forty minutes on the school bus to get to school—another thirty to forty minutes to return home. I would barely see my mother because she returned from work late. We would repeat the routine all over again the next day. I felt I did not belong. I missed my relatives from Cuiabá. I missed the warm weather. I missed being a child with my cousins. It was hard. My mother did not like Sao Paulo either. We couldn't adapt to Sao Paulo and vice versa. It was cold, busy, loud, and empty. My mother worked excessively to provide me and my siblings with a better future. But Sao Paulo was not for us.

I essentially camouflaged my emotions for the greater purpose of adapting, belonging, and trying to match my new environment.

You may be asking yourself—*Ladyane, how did you ride these emotional waves as a child? Why did you feel like you needed to belong?*

I was very little when I left my hometown. I changed schools countless times. I did not nurture childhood friendships. My childhood was unusual. So, it is only natural that I felt like I was constantly trying to adapt to the changes in my life. Almost as if trying to catch up with so many changes. This constant need to adapt also created a necessity to feel like I belonged (remember the speech? Making decisions out of *necessity* and not of options). The constant effort to adapt to the changes forced upon me as a child was always aiming to bring me this feeling of *Phew, I finally belong*. I needed to make all that effort worth something.

I guess an animal comes to mind; let's consider the chameleon, shall we? Chameleons change their colors wherever they go to match their environment. Assimilating, adapting, and camouflaging. Feeling like I belonged was essential to me because of my constant *necessity* to adapt, to adjust to all changes, and match to my new environment. Ultimately, my need to adapt impacted my ability to ride my emotional waves in a healthy manner. I did not want to cause stress to my mother—she's had enough to deal with in her life. I just wanted to adapt to the new life, make the most of it, and feel like I belonged. Is this the healthiest way to ride an emotional wave? I do not think so—you see, by camouflaging my feelings out of the necessity to adapt and match to my environment, I did nothing but worsen the atypical experiences in my life. It was a sort of bandage. I covered the scar, but the wound was still festering. I essentially camouflaged my emotions for the greater purpose of adapting, belonging, and trying to match my new environment.

So, Ladyane, did you not truly ride these emotional waves as a child? Bingo! I did not. How could I? How could a child ride an emotional wave without guidance from someone more mature? How can you do something like this as a child, when you do not have the knowledge or the tools?

You see, after years of therapy, I learned that riding the emotional wave requires learning oneself. It demands a great deal of self-awareness. To me, riding the emotional wave is only possible when I can accept and validate my own emotions. None of which I had a clue on how to do as a child. So off I went; I patched these emotions to the best of my ability and went on with my life, always trying to blend in and adapt, just like a chameleon—reacting to the changes rather than navigating and embracing them.

Chapter 3

SACRIFICES & THE BATTLEFIELD

I decide to initiate changes, embrace them, and commit to them. One wave at a time.

T HERE ARE TWO POINTS I wanted to share with you that were influential in my decision to leave Brazil.

But before I share them with you, may I please ask you to consider the word sacrifice with a different lens? I ask this because the word sacrifice generally has a negative connotation. When someone mentions the word sacrifice, one may picture pain and hurt, and it may be because when you google its definition, the words *"slaughtering"* and *"surrendering"* come up—pretty heavy, right?

Should we look at it differently? Shall we look at it through the life-journey lens? Let's look at it with a greater purpose in mind. How about: *"Sacrifice is a noble act of willingly giving something up for a greater purpose."* Is that not good enough?

Okay, so let us try this: *"Sacrifice is a testament to personal growth, fulfillment, and strength for deep transformation."* Is that a bit more uplifting? Is it not cutting it yet? Okay.

Instead, let's try this one: *"Ultimately, a sacrifice is not a loss. It is, instead, a profound and rewarding act that shows commitment, strength, resilience, compassion, and dedication, which enables you to transcend through a journey of self-awareness and transformation for the greater purpose in life."* Does this one sound a bit better? Less heavy, right? Let's go with this one—you won't regret it.

My transformation began when I left Brazil, and I started the journey of learning how to truly ride my emotional waves. Sacrifice does not sound so bad after all, right?

First, I needed to allow my expectations and reality to coexist harmoniously. To me, the relationship between my expectations and my actual reality had always been a battlefield until I reached a certain age and achieved things I have always wanted. Before that harmony, it was all a battle between both expectations and reality colliding with each other. When you think about it, though, many of our relationships today, work, marital, and friendships, have to do with managing reality and expectations, right?

It was as if my expectations and reality could not coexist in harmony for a long time. Both of them, my own set of expectations and my reality, show the same attributes but with different purposes. Imagine this:

My Expectations (The ideal scenario)—"I will stay in Brazil and figure everything out here, and it will work out. Sure, I will be able to have a great stable future here with endless career possibilities and financial stability."

Reality—trying to constantly trick me into thinking that despite all the challenges and the lack of concrete possibilities for my future, I would forever be where I was and that there was nothing I could do about it. Do you see how problematic this is? Hence, a battlefield.

Which wins, expectation or reality? Neither. I needed to make the sacrifice of leaving my home country. I also needed to create a new harmony between expectations and reality to begin exiting the life I did not want. I accepted that the decisions I needed to make were made out of necessity. However, I knew that it was precisely through my sacrifices that I was about to start paving the way to something extraordinary. Each sacrifice we make in life is a testament to our unwavering commitment to personal growth and fulfillment.

When I left Brazil to try a new life in the US, I was committed to a greater purpose because I wanted to unlock the doors to my personal growth, self-fulfillment, potential and, ultimately, start initiating the life I have always wanted. Trust me, if you are sure of your path, the direction you want to go, or the direction you want to avoid, you are halfway through the journey, and sacrificing will sound okay. Keep these new lenses in mind because I will later share with you another extraordinary sacrifice I had to make for a greater purpose. I would do it all over again in a heartbeat.

Shall we go back to my battlefield? I adjusted my expectations, faced my reality, and accepted them both. Here is what happened: I understood that my reality was not great, that for me to pursue something more significant in life (which was then my new expectation), I needed to make a few sacrifices—in this case, the sacrifice was to leave Brazil. Leaving your homeland is a complex endeavor, especially when you are about to begin your young adult life. I left everything, and the result was the creation of several gaps—cultural, emotional, family, and friendships. Migrating to a different country ultimately creates an emotional gap that we, immigrants, must learn to live with. We learn to identify and accept the gap. We learn the ability to cope with it and manage it. We then allow emotional space for that gap to exist without sorrow or pain. It is not easy, it takes time and practice. It takes mindfulness and self-awareness. It takes courage.

Once I adjusted my expectations and allowed them to coexist harmoniously with my reality, I set the course for my new beginning. I did not let my reality and experiences this far in life define who I was or what I could expect of myself and the changes yet to come, which brings me to my second point.

I like to believe that people are the way they are because of their unique journeys and not despite them. I could have chosen to complain about my life's unfortunate circumstances and how they shaped me as an adult and always say, "I cannot even speak English and can barely afford rent. How could I possibly think about leaving Brazil?" I did not think this way, though. Instead, I chose to embrace the following mantra: Because of the experiences and challenges I have encountered throughout my life, I always prefer to be a healthier version of myself. I choose to learn. I choose to grow. And I choose to take care of myself. I decide to initiate changes, embrace them, and commit to them. One step at a time. One wave at a time.

Many personal transformations come from several life experiences that shake our core foundation. Most importantly, most personal transformation results from overcoming our fears and worries. Of exercising patience and commitment intermittently. Of cultivating and nurturing self-awareness. So, what better way of growing personally than challenging yourself for a greater purpose? Use your life experiences as a school. Reflect and learn from life experiences with the ultimate goal of becoming a better version of yourself. Take advantage of these experiences. After all, we cannot control what has happened—we cannot delete unfortunate life circumstances from our lives. But we can reflect on them, learn from them, and use them to be better versions of ourselves.

Chapter 4

THE LAND OF OPPORTUNITY

You are reinventing yourself and challenging yourself despite all the challenges you have already faced in life, and for that, praise yourself.

C OMPREHENDING AND ACCEPTING THE truth of leaving Brazil was hard. The truth was that no matter how much I tried to carve out a possibility of having a better life in Brazil (which I so much tried), I was still not able to see the prospect of enjoying a career, having financial stability, owning my own home, and so many other wishes in my never-ending wish list. How would I, an 18-year-old fresh out of high school, ever enjoy all these things working as a bilingual receptionist at a law firm?

I did not want to leave Brazil. But I needed to. I needed to leave and hoped this would work despite all the challenges. Understanding that I needed to leave my country and home to try a new life somewhere else where I did not speak the language and knew nobody but my older sister was scary. So, I rode the wave right through it. However, I do not believe

I rode the wave the healthiest way; I did not know any better. Here is what the healthy way would sound like—this is what today's Ladyane would have told younger Ladyane:

"Listen, girl, give it a try and see if it works. If it doesn't, nothing is forever. You can keep on trying and change a few things on the way. Or, you can reassess your plan and strategies. Break your goals down into smaller chunks and take them one at a time. Take deep slow breaths in between. Meditate. When you finally learn how to pronounce a word correctly after countless practice sessions in front of the mirror, give yourself a pat on the back—this is hard work paying off. Give yourself a pat on the back if you nurture new friendships. Give yourself a pat on the back at the end of each day because you are at least trying. You are reinventing yourself and challenging yourself despite all the challenges you have already faced in life, and for that, praise yourself."

Friend, I did not have any of that. I was getting by without validating many of my emotions. I was hustling—I did not have time to understand my insecurities, validate them, and accept them. At that point, my small goal was to study hard and get excellent grades and a high GPA (Grade Point Average) to be able to apply for scholarships and fellowships. You must be asking yourself: "So, did it work? Did you get the scholarships and fellowships?" Yes, I did! But it was not easy. I am not sure if today it is still this way, but back then, this misconception went something like this: "If you are an international student pursuing your college degree in the US, it's because you have money." Not me. I did not have any. So why do it then? Because this was the option I wanted to see and explore. It was the only option I wanted to take a risk on.

Do you remember I mentioned finding our purpose and making decisions out of necessity? I was so young and did not have a promising future had I stayed in Brazil. My thought process was that leaving Brazil would be difficult, but I was willing to exchange the comfort and safety of remaining in my home country for a greater purpose. I truly believe that sitting on my chair today and writing this book is a testament that sacrificing something is an act that will ultimately lead to a reward.

Let's dive deeper into the unique challenges of being an international student from a third-world country in the US—are you ready? As I walk you through the cultural, financial, legal, and academic challenges, I truly hope you can relate to one or all of these challenges. I rightly believe that the way I rode the fears associated with all these challenges ignited the determination to overcome them. This sounds like magic, right? It is magical. Nonetheless, there was a lot of hard work involved.

When I decided to leave Brazil, there was no such thing as a textbook to say what I should and should not do entering the US as an international student. My older sister moved to the US when I was still a child and had just graduated from college in the US when I graduated from high school in Brazil. She offered to help me navigate the complex visa process by being my financial sponsor on paper so that I could maintain my legal status as an international student in the US. Obtaining and maintaining legal status as an international student in the US can be stressful and time-consuming. There were countless trips to the international student office on campus and countless bank statements to show we could afford the costly international student tuition—obtaining and maintaining a legal status as an international student was challenge number one for me. However, the biggest challenges were the financial constraints and the language barrier, which initially affected my academic performance.

NYC Was a Dream!

In 2005, I graduated from high school and left Brazil shortly after. I lived in a studio apartment with my older sister in Brooklyn, NYC, for a couple of months. I had a plan, which was simple but difficult to execute. I wasn't afraid, I was excited. The plan was as follows: I would attend an ESL (English as Second Language) school for a few months to improve my English and get myself ready to apply for college. In the meantime, I would have a side hustle to expose myself to the language and culture and pay for my essential expenses. For me, the best part was living with my older sister—I looked up to her, and she was my role model. She showed me around. She taught me how to get around the city that never sleeps. She took me to different places, from the Bronx to Queens and The Hamptons, and in between; I loved NYC and experiencing it with her.

I will be honest: during my honeymoon phase with NYC, I used to imagine myself in a movie set—you know, walking around 5th Avenue, crossing Central Park. It was an absolute dream! Friend, I come from a small town called Cuiabá, remember? NYC was a dream! I truly cherished the bonding time with my sister, too; we got to know each other deeply, given that I was so little when she left Brazil. It was fun. We would drink beer in our tiny Brooklyn apartment and start speaking English with each other so that I could practice. I loved it.

Sister: "No, No. Here is how you say it: 'ECZATLY'"

Ladyane: "EXXZATLY"

My diction when attempting to say "exactly" would improve with each beer we had. Who am I kidding? I was having a blast. It took me years to nail the pronunciation, but I am proud to say I eventually did. Hooray! My kids still correct my pronunciation, especially when I say "years" and "ears." We have a lot of fun.

Even though my older sister had just started her demanding career on Wall Street and worked long hours, the little time we spent together meant the world to me. Being alone in a different country, surrounded by a foreign language and no one to connect with, would have been much more challenging without my sister. I was grateful for that little time we spent together. Knowing we were both pursuing similar goals but tracing different paths comforted me. Our shared story during my early days living in the US created a deep understanding and empathy, creating a solid foundation for us to support each other, especially during challenging times. I truly love this unique aspect of my relationship with my older sister—what we lived through, the happy and sad memories, helped us create a connection that will never fade away.

Friend, NYC made me feel like I could fit in. I felt like I belonged to the city that never sleeps. I made so many friends, some of whom I keep in touch with today.

Like the chameleon, I assimilated the culture and adapted; I camouflaged and blended right in—with my thick accent, but I did. NYC brought the best out of me. I felt motivated and excited about the new future I was starting. I felt like a sponge, trying my best to learn and adapt. Did I miss my mother? Yes. Did I miss my childhood friends? Yes. But I was motivated to learn and to grow. My purpose was clear back then: *I am here because this new endeavor will allow me to be financially stable. I will create a better life for myself and my family.* So I kept on going.

But it wasn't always this clear. Along the way, I crossed paths with some incredible people who opened my eyes to new possibilities and perspectives on how I could succeed as an immigrant in the US. The supporting village I built empowered me to seize every opportunity during my early days in this country.

The Accent Fear Becomes My Close Friend

*Accents are true reflections of diversity, heritage,
and identity—all relevant aspects in life for carrying on personal values.*

I had to take an ESL class during my first college semester. That's because I did not get a high enough score on my college-entry assessment exam, so I needed to improve my English. Even though today I realized taking this ESL class was the best thing that could have happened to me during my first semester in college in the US, I initially got furious for having to pay an international student tuition for an ESL class — any cent I could save back then was a win for me given that I did not have much.

In this class, I met my outstanding ESL professor. Thanks to my ESL professor, I learned to overcome one of the first challenges I faced in America—accent fear. She once told me, "It is okay to have an accent as long as you speak and write proper and correct English." I thought to myself, *I can do that!*

**Surround yourself with those who empower you on
some level. Create your supporting environment.**

I do not know if she understands how immensely relevant and reas-suring those words were to me back then. My ESL professor empow-ered me. She made me feel confident. And I will forever be grateful for her kind and wise words. Shortly after that, there was no *"accent fear"* anymore. Accent fear became more of a buddy, a close friend. All because of what my ESL professor had said to me. And now I ask you —how important is it to surround yourself with those who uplift and inspire you on some level? I will tell you, it makes a significant difference for me. And I try to be that person to my friends and loved ones, too. It's a two-way street. Having people who share similar values inspire and motivate us without asking for anything in return is truly a gift. Surround yourself with those who empower you on some level. Create your supporting environment. Riding the many emotional waves that would come my way as an immigrant was a bit less challenging because I learned the importance of creating a supporting village filled with people who could provide me with some support and understood my purpose. This shows that having a supporting village before motherhood is vital for our personal growth.

After my ESL professor's wise words, I never tried to hide my accent. I would bravely raise my hand in a classroom with 100+ students and speak up. I accepted my accent. I never wanted to hide it and I do not get offended when someone asks me where my accent is from. I get pretty excited and proudly reply with a big smile, "*It's from Brazil!*"

Friend, I must be bluntly honest with you right now—we cannot control how people perceive us and the box they so arrogantly try to fit us in. Instead, how about we try to remember this:

The necessity to label someone based on one's accent is merely a misconception and projection of prejudice, all of which we have no control over.

The label and the preconceived opinion people may have about you due to your accent do not define your abilities, knowledge, and character. Instead, accents are true reflections of diversity, heritage, and identity—all relevant aspects in life for carrying on personal values.

Transitioning and building a new life in a new country with a new culture, language, and relationships is far from simple. The cultural assimilation, the language barrier, keeping a legal immigration status, discrimination, and stereotypes are just a few of the challenges I faced. But friend, do you want to know the truth? Some things will never go away. Another lesson I learned is that there are a few close-minded people out there who still need to fit me in a little box so they can feel superior, and there is absolutely nothing I can do about that. It is out of my control. But what I can and choose to do is appreciate the transformation process these challenges caused in me. The first transformation is to accept your accent and move on with your goals. Here is how I look at it:

I speak more than one language—this makes me smart. If someone decides to label me and fit me into a limited box because of my accent or where I come from, I will choose my box, which would be the smart box.

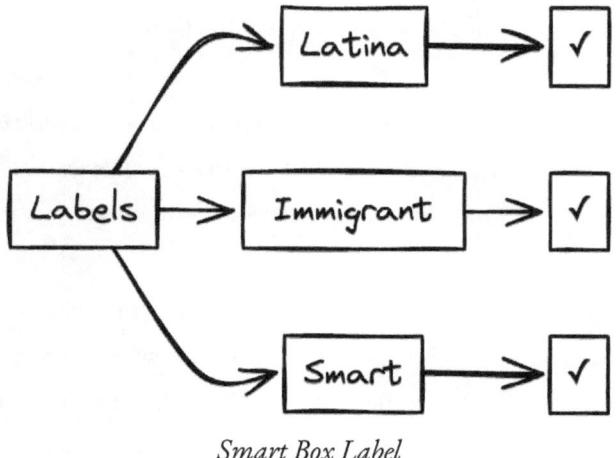

Smart Box Label

The College Life: The Surprising Distraction & The Search for Money

My academic life in the US can be divided into two phases. Initially, I had the scarcity phase, which meant I was broke, counted coins, and had no scholarships or fellowships. The second phase is the abundance phase, where I was paid to study. How did I go from scarcity to abundance as an international student in the US? Hang tight—this gets interesting.

The first phase could have been more pleasant. The financial constraints I faced during the first two years of my academic career in college were nerve-racking. I was stressed, lost weight, and barely ate. I lived in the college library. I took classes during the day and headed to the library at night to study to get good grades and apply for merit-based scholarships and fellowships. But there was another problem; only a few institutions were willing to fund international students in the US back then. If I were to guess, the predominant assumption was that international students can afford the expensive college tuition. I was an exception to the rule. This financial constraint drained me. I was constantly stressed, on high alert, counting coins, and exhausted by the thought of not being able to finish my college education in the US.

Fortunately, during my first year, with the help of a supportive family friend, I got a small student loan to help me get by with the essential expenses—rent, food, books, transportation, and phone bills. I quickly learned a useful trick about my books. As soon as the professor displayed the class syllabus, which listed all the books needed for that particular class, I would borrow them from the library and renew the book loan during the entire semester so that I would not have to pay for the book. I was glad I could save some money on that front. I must confess that borrowing books from the library became a habit even during my abundance phase. I couldn't help myself.

At that point, I was still living with my sister, but our lifestyles were different, so I decided to rent a small bedroom in Astoria, Queens. It was a good decision because we both needed our individual spaces in different life phases. During that year, I used the loan money to focus on my studies to get a high GPA and apply for merit-based scholarships and fellowships. I used to have a side hustle, and with that money, I paid for my daily coffee in the cafeteria on campus. I had a budget, and I stuck with it.

What did college life look like for me? No dorm. No on-campus life. I would wake up early, take classes during the day, go to work, and then return to campus in the evening to take more classes or study in the library. I would stay in the library, sometimes past midnight. Next day: all over again. I would study in my bedroom on weekends or head to the library. I invested all my brain capacity in my studies. I was active on campus, volunteered, and always participated in all classes. Each professor knew who I was, regardless of the class size. I was always curious and eager to learn. Professors liked that, and they would go beyond their office hours to chat with me. I would always follow up with a thank-you note. On weekends, I would lose track of time while studying and miss a meal or two. Eventually, I realized I was transforming again. I realized I was an intense person. But what do I mean by *intense* exactly? I would allow myself to play a bit and hang out with friends. Still, I was so determined to excel in my studies that I focused my energy, emotion, and brain capacity on pursuing my goal. I invested my time in pursuing my purpose.

My long-term goal was to graduate with a guaranteed job in a company that could apply for my job visa. My short-term goal was to get good grades and merit-based scholarships to finish my college education. These goals were crystal clear to me, so I was focused, determined, driven, and passionate about my reality. Today's Ladyane thinks not having too many distractions helped her invest in these goals with intention and clarity. Pause. Hang on a second— what would college life be like without a college sweetheart? The only consistent distraction that got me through college with a bit of fun and butterflies in my stomach had a name. Noah, my best friend and husband, became my emotional anchor in the US.

The Surprising Distraction

Noah and I met in January 2008 during that ESL class I mentioned to you. At first, I thought he was annoying but funny. He would always have an opinion and make sure to speak up. He and I often went back and forth during class, respectfully disagreeing on some exciting topics. I liked hearing him talk—what can I say? I have a sweet spot for his Israeli accent. We had friends in common, and so we became friends too. He was an interesting guy. His life narrative excited me; he took classes and worked simultaneously. He knew what he wanted and worked tirelessly to get it (sound familiar? Hint: she is writing this book). His journey was attractive to me. His sharpness and sense of humor made me fall for him. We developed a friendship, and soon enough, he went from merely interesting to a super attractive, hot Israeli friend.

Life plays some tricks on us, right? His story fascinated me—he was born and raised in Israel, he was Jewish, and an army veteran. He moved to the US to try a new life. We had that in common, too. And while we came from two completely different worlds, we realized we were pretty alike and enjoyed each other's humor. We had the same taste in music and shared our favorite movie quotes. Did I tell you he played the guitar? Yes! He does it to this day. Noah and I started dating in September of 2008 and we have been together ever since.

The Supporting Village Does Not Begin in Motherhood

We should start building our supporting village before motherhood.

As a college student in the US, I cherished the abundance of opportunities available, from the vast resources to the one-to-one meetings with my mentors. College was a place where I truly felt I belonged. The day I interviewed for the FWA-Baruch Mentorship Program will always be in my memory. Being part of this mentorship program changed everything for me. I will tell you more or less how it happened.

The FWA-Baruch Mentoring Program was established at Baruch College around the early 2000s, and the Program's core is a one-to-one mentorship between female executive mentors and female students as mentees. To qualify as a mentee, students must meet specific criteria, including maintaining a GPA of 3.5 or higher, demonstrating academic excellence, and participating in extracurricular activities. I met all of them. But I still doubted myself. FWA helped me stop doubting myself. Do you remember when I told you that a supporting village is not limited to motherhood? I started building my supporting village right there as a FWA mentee.

As I walked into a fancy hotel lobby in Manhattan, Suzan and Beth, the women representing the FWA-Baruch Mentorship Program and responsible for interviewing and recruiting mentees, were waiting to interview me to join the mentorship program. I was nervous—again, the imposter syndrome kicking in. The monologue in my head repeating the same questions: *What if they don't like me? What if they decide I do not have what it takes to be a FWA mentee? I need this so much! I really want this. Okay, Ladyane, breathe in and out.* There I was, young Ladyane, riding an emotional wave.

The application consisted of completing a form, writing an essay telling them why I deserved to be an FWA mentee, and meeting with Suzan and Beth for an in-person interview. The three of us sat in the hotel lobby, and they eased me into the interview. I felt my heart racing with each word coming out of my mouth, imposter syndrome coming back: *What if they can't understand me because of my accent?* I immediately thought of my ESL teacher and what she told me about accents. I told them I wanted to graduate with honors, and that I wanted to launch my career on Wall Street. I told them I wasn't sure which area yet, but I hoped FWA could guide me through all the options. I told them my life story and how I was in the process of applying for scholarships and fellowships. I think they liked what they were hearing, because they had follow-up comments and smiles on their faces. I was accepted to the program and matched with a fantastic mentor, Sophia Luthernan.

Sophia was a top executive at a multinational technology and consulting company — I couldn't think of a better role model and mentor for me. She was so put together, intelligent, and elegant. I am not joking when I tell you I wanted to be her when I grew up. She taught me how to be more put together. Don't get me wrong, there was nothing wrong with how I was. The idea was that I wanted to be more polished professionally. I did not have to change my personality, but I tried to be polished and professional when networking or speaking with a top executive. I wanted to be perceived differently, not just as a Latina student but as an intelligent, go-getter, doer Latina executive. I learned with her that for me to have a career in the US, I needed to work on my cultural assimilation; this required adaptability, cultural sensitivity, and willingness to embrace new experiences and ways of working. It required a lot of observing. One day, she invited me to shadow her in her office as she went about her typical workday. (The idea of "shadowing" someone at work for a few hours in the day is to encourage learning by observing a more experienced professional execute their daily work.). It was amazing! Shadowing her opened my eyes to what I could become professionally. She was my role model—I wanted to be just like her when I finally entered the job market. Do you see how powerful this is? It goes back to having a supporting village—we should start building our supporting village before motherhood.

Supporting Village Vision Board

Our fulfillment and empowerment have never been
so important than today—solely because now we
have the tools we once lacked to foster a more inclu-
sive, diverse, and prosperous path for ourselves.

The term "supporting village" is excessively used in the context of motherhood nowadays. I do not recall hearing or reading this term in any other context. Friend, it's time for us to change that. We must start creating our supporting villages way before motherhood, doing so will bring fulfillment and a solid foundation for us not to get lost and overwhelmed with the many roles we deserve and work hard to play. It will enable us to live our best life. It is not too late to create one if you do not have one yet. We can start creating that village, and here is how: Surround yourself with those who can add to you in different aspects of your life, from sharing different resources to connecting emotionally. From those who add to your personal growth to those who are role models. From those who ask the right questions to those who provide you a sense of comfort and safety during challenging times.

As you transform, your supporting village may change. The Ladyane who arrived in the US in 2006 is not the one from today, and there are a few people who kept their roles in my village, but some left and made room for others. And that's okay. My village today comprises a particular group of people—from family members to friends, from sponsors in different areas to mentors from all backgrounds. They helped shape the former Wall Street executive into a mother of three, fulfilled and determined to ignite inspiration and empowerment among women everywhere. So, if my supporting village did this to me, yours will do the same—whatever the change you're going through. Whatever your purpose turns out to be. Your supporting village will cherish your change and support you all the way.

Our fulfillment and empowerment have never been so important than today, solely because now we have the tools we once lacked to foster a more inclusive, diverse, and prosperous path for ourselves. One in which we can create balance and use it in our favor. I know it is easier said than done, but if we care for ourselves by surrounding ourselves with those who appreciate our journey, everything will fall into place. We have a lot of work to do, but we cannot do it alone. As women, we play many well-deserved roles and need a supporting village. And this needs to happen before motherhood. Now, take a moment—think about where you are and where you want to be. And, ask yourself, how do I want my supporting village to look like today?

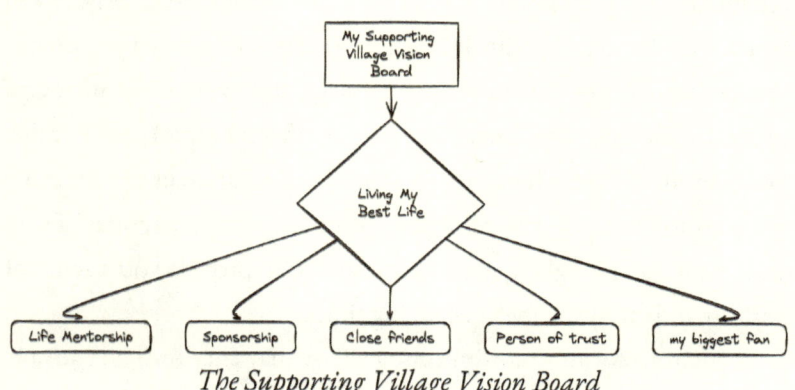

The Supporting Village Vision Board

Designing My Major & The Labels We Fit In

*How about we use the labels society thrusts upon us
as symbols of the challenges we face and obstacles
we overcome? How about we use these labels as a
representation of personal growth?*

One of the best things that happened to me during my college career in the US was being a City University New York Baccalaureate (CUNY BA) Program student. The program is part of the CUNY system and allows independent minds to design their majors based on their interests and passions. This program encourages students to work closely with academic mentors to design their majors by choosing top classes within the several senior CUNY colleges. How amazing is this, right? Back then, I had multiple interests and couldn't decide on one field over the other, so I worked closely with two outstanding professors from Baruch College to design my major. I graduated with honors in Political Science.

I used to meet monthly with my mentors to discuss class curriculums and how they could align with my interests. I had one mentor in the Political Science Department and another in the Finance/Economics Department. I would sit down with them, and they would guide me through the unknowns of academia. They suggested specific paths for nurturing skills with the top goal in mind—making the best out of the CUNY BA Program and leveraging the amazing classes and professors at Baruch College. My academic mentors became part of my supporting village.

Before every meeting with my academic mentors, I prepared myself the best I could. I knew they were busy and used their regular teaching hours to meet with me. So I needed to be sharp and not waste their time; at least, that's how I saw it. I wanted to be on top of my game. I had a one-liner about the classes I was taking and what I liked and disliked the most in each one of them. I prepared a one-liner about the assignments and projects I was working on for each class I was taking. I wanted them to see that their time guiding me was worth it. In one of these meetings, my Political Science mentor threw a surprising and scary question at me: "Why don't you write an honors thesis?" At first, I thought I misunderstood what she said. I then realized I understood the question but was speechless. Nothing could come out of my mouth. I could not believe she asked me that question. But before I answered, I quickly thought *Does she believe I am good enough to write an honors thesis? How is this even possible?* And so, in disbelief, I asked: "Do you think I can do it?" And she said confidently: "I not only think you can do it, but I think you will do amazing."

My Political Science mentor had a star in my supporting village vision board because she became my academic role model. She mentored me for one year while I wrote my ninety-three-page-long senior honors thesis in Political Science. Twelve years later, I had recently met with her and she said: "I always thought you would do great in academia, but I knew you had other aspirations back then." How amazing is it to hear from your role model and college mentor that she thought you could be like her one day? It is amazing to know that if you work hard, you can overcome obstacles. It is fulfilling to know your supporting village cherishes your journey.

On April 30, 2012, I delivered my honors thesis. On May 8, 2012, I presented the thesis to the Committee on Undergraduate Honors of Baruch College, and in June 2012, I graduated with honors in Political Science. Graduating with honors as an immigrant in the US started an emotional turmoil in me. When I started college in the US, I was taken by mixed feelings of fear, stress, and anxiety. These feelings changed as time passed, as I started succeeding in my academic endeavor — being the recipient of a fellowship and, ultimately, having a successful summer internship in a global investment bank enabled me to feel more confident, hopeful, less afraid, and less anxious. Eventually, at my college graduation, I felt fulfilled. Graduating with honors was like having another label followed by a checkmark in that list of labels we discussed.

Do you know what I realized during the process of personal transformation? The more labels, the better; we are evolving and growing. Hear me out: Labels are ways for people to categorize us in society. But for us, those who go through personal transformation, these labels mean much more. They have emotional weight. They have a history. They have tears of sadness and joy. How about we use the labels society thrusts upon us as symbols of the challenges we face and obstacles we overcome? How about we use these labels as a representation of personal growth? Markers of individual resilience and evolution? I argue that the more labels, the better for us.

Let's turn labels into our vision board!

Let's benefit from these labels.

Let's be proud.

So, let there be more labels. Little did I know back in 2008 that in less than seven years, I would have a checkmark on three other new labels—a Wall Street Vice President, a Jewish woman, and a mother.

The Search for Money & The Journey Is Not a Race

*Instead of comparing ourselves to others, we should
focus on our path, embracing each experience as a
chance to learn and evolve.*

Shall we go back to the search for money? What a curious title for this
section of the book. As I write this, I think: *Should I change it?* and *What
does searching for money even mean?*

Growing up, my "search for money," or managing the lack of it,
became part of my life and that of my family. It is safe to say that my new
life in the US was all about pursuing financial stability. But for you to
understand why this search became my purpose for a long time, I need
to take you back to my childhood.

While my father was still alive, we had ups and downs financially.
There was a time when we had multiple houses in different cities, cars
parked in the garage, parties, and trips. We had a vacation home, and
my mom always wore the best outfits and jewelry. Our house had a
huge playground, and a beautiful pool shaped like a water bottle—the
same pool my father taught me how to swim when I was still a baby.
However, suddenly, overnight, we had nothing. And it was difficult. No
warning. No planning. All the money we had disappeared from our bank
accounts.

In the early 90s, Brazil was going through an economic crisis. Inflation
was through the roof. The political scenario was catastrophic. Brazil
had just gone through over 20 years of military dictatorship. President
Fernando Collor was democratically elected in 1989. You are thinking:
Well, that's good. At least there is no more dictatorship. Not so fast. The
day after Collor took office, he simply confiscated everyone's money

without warning. No one saw it coming. He did not tell Brazilians what his plans were. Or rather, he hid his plans from Brazilians. Just like that, the money disappeared. Imagine you go to sleep, and your money still belongs to you, safe in the bank. The next day, you wake up, your money disappears, and you have nothing. At that time, he claimed he did it to fight inflation and encourage economic stability. Instead, he created panic—pure chaos. People committed suicide; all the money Brazilians had worked so hard to earn simply disappeared. Can you imagine? The same happened to us. My mom tells me that many years of hard and intense work evaporated. My parents went into desperation mode. We went from having everything to having nothing overnight. Collor resigned from the presidency in 1992. And we still had nothing.

Shortly after the money was gone, my father's health started declining. His drinking problems became worse. Today, in retrospect, I think stress played an important role in the deterioration of his health. We moved to the big city for better opportunities a few years after he passed. Later on, pursuing a better life, which included financial security, led me to leave my home country and move to the US.

Now, what does the search for money in college look like? It involves hunting for scholarships and fellowships.

After a full year of hard work, I achieved a high GPA and started searching for scholarships, fellowships, and grants. This search was like having a full-time job, except that I did not get bi-weekly paychecks, nor did I have a manager. The search was also frustrating because only some institutions were funding international students. At one point, I juggled full-time classes, a part-time job on campus, a scholarship search, volunteering activities, and a babysitting gig I had, all at once. I did not have much time left for me. I was okay with that, though—I knew hard work would pay off, and I was focused on my purpose.

So, friend, if you are reading this and thinking of trying your college career in the US or sending your son or daughter to the US to pursue his/her college education, I wanted to share the lessons I have learned. But before I go ahead and do it, please allow me to share the most important one, which would have saved me some sleepless nights. For a long time, we are conditioned to associate racing with mostly everything we pursue—think about it. Getting good grades is a race. Becoming the top of your class is a race. Being the best student is a race. You are racing to make your team's best employee of the month. You are racing to register your son or daughter to the most popular summer camp. You are racing to send birthday invitations. You are racing to make a good impression. Inevitably, you end up comparing yourself to others. But you do not have control over what others do or think. So then this becomes a cycle that never ends. Sometimes, this cycle leaves us frustrated and hopeless; again, we have little or no control over it.

What if I told you the pursuit of whatever you set yourself to do is not a race? It isn't a walk in the park, either. Pursuing that something great you have been aiming for is more like riding a wave—there will be challenges and big emotions. There may be tears of joy and sadness, but it is just you and the waves. No one else. Instead of comparing ourselves to others, we should focus on our path, embracing each experience as a chance to learn and evolve. Ultimately, I want to feel fulfilled and happy; it can only happen if I control my ride. I am the one who needs to overcome my obstacles: my fears, challenges, and shortcomings. Not anyone else. I am the one in the driver's seat. I promise you, friend, if you think this way, magic will happen because you will control your ride. Now that we have covered this piece, it is time to share a few lessons I learned in college. I took control of my financial stability in college. I didn't care that there weren't many institutions funding international students. I did not care that my classmates paid less than half of what I paid for tuition. I did not care if she or he spoke English without an accent. I did what I had to do; I found the money and eventually got paid to attend college.

I wish I could have written here that I was a good athlete and had a scholarship because of that, but I could not. My best place was at the library rather than the swimming pool or the basketball court. I never did well in sports competitions and thought my physical attributes did not help me much on that—that's true until today. For lack of a better comparison, finding scholarships and fellowships were like finding a needle in a haystack. So here is how I was able to afford it. Put it up on your vision board, girl!

Number one: I got myself very organized. Every day between classes and at night, I would dedicate time to research for grants. I documented my research in a spreadsheet and searched the internet for scholarships/fellowships databases, because it saved me time when I needed to apply for several grants simultaneously—all the information I needed was in one location, which was easy to understand and work with. I created the spreadsheet myself, and if my memory doesn't fail me, the column headings were something like this: Financial Aid Type (options were scholarship or fellowship), the next column: Criteria/Requirements, next: Minimum GPA, next: Website Link, Application Deadline, and Application Submitted (Yes/No).

Now, in a nutshell, the main difference between scholarships and fellowships is that if you receive a fellowship, you do not need to keep applying for it every semester—all you need to do is to keep showing academic excellence. With a scholarship, on the other hand, you need to apply every semester or every year all over again. So, in theory, a fellowship may be better. But any money I could receive to support my academic pursuit was something especially considering the international student tuition cost.

Number two: Be bold and generous about describing yourself and your academic work in your fellowship/scholarship applications. *What do I mean by that?* Showcase your strengths. Don't be shy. Don't sell yourself short. Be specific about your academic experience; if it relates to the scholarship/fellowship requirements, that's a bonus! Show your aspirations—write about what you would do if granted the award. Tell them your story and how it connects to the relevant award; this led me to create one application for each scholarship and each fellowship I applied for. The search was like a full-time job. Hard work pays off.

Number three: Search for a research study grant. I created a spreadsheet and searched for research grants. I landed a research study on a sociology topic with one of my first college professors. The grant allowed me to learn a great deal of research skills, and I was paid to do it. It boosted my confidence. Think about it: I was doing research work from the comfort of the college library or my home, and someone was paying me for it. How cool!

Shortly after submitting several scholarships and fellowship applications, I received the Thomas W. Smith Academic Fellowship. It was a remarkable moment during my college career in the US. The Thomas W. Smith Fellowship is granted to CUNY BA students who maintain a GPA of 3.5 or higher and show academic excellence. Being awarded this fellowship gave me a profound sense of validation and accomplishment—many years of hard work, second-guessing my decisions that far in life, and asking if it was all worth it. The award made me feel like I belonged to a unique group of intelligent and hard-working students. There I was, being called to go up on the stage as a Thomas W. Smith Fellow. A quick snapshot of life memories went through my head:

A little girl running around the big house that she lost when her father passed.

A little girl living in her godparents' house because there was no other place to go.

A little girl moving from a small town to a big city.

A young girl arrives in New York City feeling nervous about her future.

Suddenly, up on that stage, my stomach settled. I could breathe. Because of my hard work and dedication, I had the money I needed to finish my college education in the US. I deserved it. I was finally achieving something I had manifested and been so intentional about.

Being awarded an academic fellowship was a transformative experience—it propelled me into a new realm of possibilities, paving the way for further personal and intellectual growth. I felt relieved. For the rest of my academic career, I did not need to worry about affording international student tuition. I could ride the wave without fear and enjoy the excitement of being awarded money to study in the US as an immigrant. There was a lot of pride. I enjoyed my new reality, and it aligned with my expectations.

But good things come in waves, and as I enjoyed my new reality, I was about to ride many good waves.

My Inaugural Gig In the US

Even the smallest opportunities could yield signif-
icant outcomes. Be vigilant - keep an eye out and
embrace them as if they were worth a fortune.

Legally, international students can only work on campus and only twenty hours per week. What did I do? I got myself an on-campus job. I searched a lot and landed a "college assistant" job that paid me $18 per hour. The job opportunity was amazing back then, given that many of the other roles paid between $12 to 15 per hour. I remember it like it was yesterday; I searched for a job in the career section of the CUNY Graduate Center website. I applied and got an invite for an interview. The day of the interview, I arrived a few minutes earlier, and there she was, my future manager, Laura. I was a nervous wreck. It was my first official job interview since I had moved to the US. *What if she asks something and I do not understand? What if she asks about my technical skills and I cannot answer? What if she thinks I have a strong accent? What if, What if, and What if.*

She introduced herself, described the role I had applied for, and asked me how to pronounce my name. I thought to myself, *She cares.* She made me feel comfortable. She was very personable. I told her a little bit about myself. She asked me a few questions like: "Are you good in Excel?" "Can you streamline the end-of-year faculty evaluation process?" I excitedly answered, "Absolutely." Did I have any idea how I was going to do that? No, but I thought I could figure something out. After a few more questions, she thanked me for my time and introduced me to David, who was responsible for faculty recruitment and development. He was a cool guy, down-to-earth, and friendly. We hit it off quickly.

Shortly after I joined the team, David and I spent a lot of time chatting about music in general, but in particular about Depeche Mode. We both loved Depeche Mode. Everyone in the office made me feel like I belonged.

The office was small. Initially, I did not have a desk; I used the desk of whoever was not in the office on a particular day. One day, Laura said we were going to be office buddies. Yes, it was my first serious job in the US, and I was sharing an office with my manager. Laura gave me a little office desk, and we placed it right next to her office door. Every day, I would come in, chat with Laura about personal things, and we would wrap it up about work. I continued with my work, but I always noticed how she spoke to people. Laura does not know this, but she became a professional role model to me. Do you know why? She was always kind yet professional. Her tone was always clear and straightforward, however, she made people feel comfortable when talking to her. So, friend, it was there, in a small office on the fifth floor of the CUNY Graduate Center building right on 5th Avenue, in the heart of Manhattan, that I started learning the skills I would need in Wall Street. A part-time college assistant job did not pay much but it started me off in the right direction. Even the smallest opportunities can yield significant outcomes. Be vigilant, keep an eye out and embrace them as if they are worth a fortune.

Friend, do you see the importance of this on-campus part-time job to me? This job was all about the opportunity. Even though $18 per hour was a tremendous help for me, this opportunity was about my exposure to the US working environment. I could not think of a better group of people to work with. I am forever thankful for them.

Embrace all opportunities that come your way.
Sharpen your senses to recognize them when they are
not obvious.

Here are a few other lessons I learned in this job: I learned the importance of selective hearing, the ability to focus on specific sounds while ignoring others. I shared an office with my manager. There were times I paid close attention to what she was saying, but there were times I did not listen to everything she said. Laura never asked me to leave the office when she discussed personal matters with her husband, for example. But I learned how to tune out when I noticed she was having this type of conversation. Selective hearing is a great skill to have on Wall Street. Why? Picture this: You have a small desk on a vast trading floor where people are talking to each other, having calls, multiple TV screens showing financial news, and you need to concentrate and can't afford to get distracted because you need to produce spotless work. How do you do it? Selective hearing! You filter irrelevant information from the relevant. So, embrace all opportunities that come your way. Sharpen your senses to recognize them when the opportunities are not obvious. I promise you that a modest professional opportunity or encounter can yield significant outcomes. I will tell you more about this when I talk about the importance of networking.

Other than selective hearing, I used this opportunity to develop foundational professional skills. I learned how to write professional emails, answer the phone, lead a meeting, and solve conflicts. I was in charge of the performance evaluations of all faculty members, and Laura let me handle it all. She would give me tips on how to communicate, and David would help me with grammar at times. I spent the rest of my sophomore, junior, and senior years in college working as a college assistant. My last day as a college assistant was May 16, 2012. My first day on Wall Street as a young Latina professional was June 11th, 2012.

The Surprising Distraction — Do All Good Things
Come to an End?

It is now 2010, and Noah and I have been dating for over two years. Things are getting more serious. The connection exists. The love is there, for sure. We didn't complete each other's sentences but rather added to each other's thoughts. We always talked and provided each other with different perspectives on things. Noah was always more relaxed than me. He always made me laugh. Noah always cheered for me and understood why I worked so hard. He worked hard, too. With that in common, we started developing a more profound connection—admiration may be the word I am looking for. We admired each other's dedication. However, with a deeper connection, there are also doubts and questions. *Where is this relationship taking us? What are we doing?* I asked. It bothered me that Noah had not introduced me to his family when they visited from Israel, given that we had been dating for over two years. *"We aren't aligned,"* I said. He agreed. But to make things a bit more challenging for us, Noah's family opposed our relationship.

At that time, his parents drew an expectation upon him, which involved Noah marrying a Bukharian Jewish girl, and if she spoke Russian, that was the cherry on top of the pie. I was far from that picture, right? Latina and far from the Jewish reality, at least at that point. The image was clear to both of us. We went our separate ways in October 2010. Neither one of us wanted it to be that way. We were both hurt and wanted more of what we could once give each other. But how could we continue? How can a son manage his parents' unrealistic expectations while still being emotionally okay? How can you navigate your parents' expectations and remain true to yourself and your feelings? What happens when your parent's expectations collide with what a son envisioned as his happily ever after? After we broke up, I focused on my studies and my search for a Wall Street internship; I needed one for the summer of 2011 so that I could have a job offer upon my graduation, which was expected to happen in May 2012. This distraction helped me. I still loved him. And he loved me.

Noah and I did not see or speak with each other for about four months. Two things were clear to me. First, I did not want and did not like to be in between a son and his parents' relationship—it did not feel right. I wanted to be a reason for happiness rather than tension. I concluded they needed to figure out their emotions and that I did not belong in that process. Second, I never agreed with the mindset of opposing a relationship solely based on cultural and religious differences. This mindset has no space in my belief system, it never did and never will. I welcome differences.

As a matter of fact, I am attracted to differences. Differences are what make us unique and special. I never resented Noah's parents, though—how could I? The environment and background in which they were raised shaped their initial reluctance to accept me into their family. Could they have chosen to question the misconception or change it? Did they ever encounter anything different from what they were accustomed to? I do not think so. They faced other challenges, other questions, and other dilemmas in life. And I have always respected that. Embracing differences and welcoming an outsider into their world was not one of the things they ever tried to do or were taught how to do—a different generation with a different belief system. But Noah and I were about to change that.

While we embraced our love story and its challenges, I also focused on keeping academic excellence and searching for money to finish my college education.

The Search For Money Continues

When I won the Thomas W. Smith Academic Fellowship, it took me a while for it to sink in, and I was in disbelief. Later, I found myself relieved. I felt proud. It did not take long for the racing thoughts to kick in; that emotional wave surrendered to fear. The racing thoughts were coming from all directions: *What would have happened if I didn't win this fellowship? How would I afford college? So many doors are opening because of this fellowship! This means so much for my academic career.* A few days later, when I finally received the check, I thought: *Now, onto the next endeavor: career.* You see, I did not stop. In retrospect, I realize that for many years, even before I moved to the US, I felt like I was sprinting downhill, desperately fleeing from the looming rock behind me, all while striving to reach a place of safety. I did not relax. This is not healthy, right? I was in this constant alert mode, always thinking there was something else I needed to do to reach the safe zone.

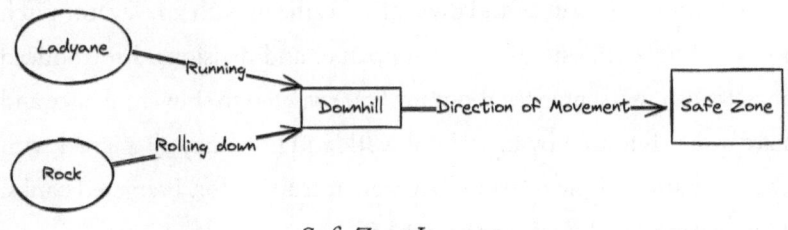

Safe Zone Journey

My next endeavor was to land myself a summer internship.

It was the fall of 2010. The college campus was getting ready for job fair days. Companies came to campus to advertise themselves and show students what they would be recruiting for the following summer. The career center played a pivotal role in this initiative. They organized job fair events, assisted students with resumé guidance, and conducted mock interviews. The career center on campus also managed a job search database from which students could benefit during their job search journey.

I took advantage of the career center and similar assistance the FWA-Baruch mentorship program offered. On this job fair day, I visited a few companies' booths, talked to some people representing the companies, and asked relevant questions. I researched the companies ahead of time. I prepared a sentence or two to start the conversation and make it enjoyable. I was networking. Afterward, I would gather the person's email address and follow up with a thank you email. LinkedIn was not as popular back then, we were still in the email era.

I did not get the internship from the job fair. The companies were not recruiting during that day; instead, they introduced themselves to the students. But I took this day as an opportunity to practice my networking skills and develop relationships. It worked.

Later in the winter of 2010, the college hosted a career fair—this was when I needed to prepare myself with a well-written resumé and my elevator pitch to make a good impression. As usual, I researched all the companies I wanted to work for, looked at what internal divisions they were recruiting for, and updated the heading of my resume to align with each of those companies and divisions. I came in with an elevator pitch prepared for each one of those companies and divisions. I introduced myself with two sentences about my life. I wanted to show resilience and hard work, followed by my school work and how they all aligned with the company and the division they were recruiting for. I targeted banks. I knew banks could sponsor my job visa.

I stopped by four to five different booths. Banks were all recruiting for different divisions: finance, operations, internal audit, and investment banking. Some even offered a scholarship and an internship opportunity. *Very generous!* I thought. For every bank, I handed one copy of my resumé, connected with the recruiter at some level, and sent a follow-up thank-you email. It felt like a race; the fair happened at the gymnasium on campus. It was a big event, and all students were after the same thing. The so-called *"Summer Internship."* The entire experience was dreadful;

most students, such as myself, were anxious about this. Everyone needed a summer internship for multiple reasons. Some wanted it because they wanted the experience in their resume. Others wanted it because of the money. Others wanted it because of the guaranteed job opportunity upon graduation, which was my case. I needed it badly.

The career fair was just the beginning of the search. Before that, I needed to prepare by researching the banks and divisions. I finished writing my resumé and reviewed it with the career center and my FWA mentor. Shortly after the fair, the application process began. Everything was through the banks' websites. After applying for each role, I emailed each of my contacts from each bank, expressed my continued interest in the opportunity, and thanked them for considering my application. The email showed enthusiasm and professionalism. Years later, when I was on the other side of this race, I kept an eye open for those students who emailed me. I think this indeed shows a go-getter attitude, which is an extraordinary quality to have in the finance industry. Or in any industry, if I am honest.

A dreadful feeling took over me as the weeks passed, and I did not get a phone call or an email about my applications. As I recall correctly, I applied to eight different banks. I luckily made it to the interview process for five banks. But during my last set of interviews, I was ready to give up. I was not successful. My confidence and self-esteem reached rock bottom. During those days, I managed countless emotional waves—so many interviews, so much preparation, and intense competition.

It was now March 2011. Banks started to interview for the summer. After disappointing interviews, I started doubting my ability to get a job on Wall Street. I doubted I was good enough for the industry, convinced I did not have what it took. Most interviews felt robotic and harsh, which left me thinking, *I am not sure I want to be part of this.*

I decided to start getting ready to pack my things and return to Brazil after graduation. While reaching desperation mode, I did not want to leave my new reality, the one I worked so hard to create for myself, which aligned with my expectations. There was too much personal growth at stake. It was just a lot of effort I did not want to leave behind. In this desperate mode, I went on another set of interviews. When I thought nothing could make me feel worse about myself, another reality check hit me right in my heart and soul.

The Summer Internship Interrogation

On this day I woke up at 5:30 a.m. I made a conscious effort to wake up earlier than I usually did to secure my turn in the shared bathroom of the Astoria house, where I rented a bedroom and shared a bathroom with three other girls. The last thing I needed that day was to be late for my interview because I did not get a turn to shower on time. I was nervous. I managed to get to the interview ahead of time. *Hey, little win for me*! I thought. They called me into the office.

Two interviewers, a female and a male, sit on one side of the meeting table. As soon as I walked in, they greeted me with a cold "Good Morning" and screened through me from top to bottom, making their way back to my face. I thought to myself: *Ow this does not help me*. I felt intimidated. They did not even say my name nor look me in the eye. *Not a good start, but let's do this,* I thought in a failed attempt to calm myself down. In a way, I was disappointed. I wasn't expecting the female interviewer to be so tough during the interview process —I assumed she wouldn't appreciate others treating her that way. It's the classic "don't do to others what you wouldn't want done to you" situation.

The interview started with them both, still not mentioning my name, introducing themselves. They took their time to glorify themselves and what they so meticulously did in each of their roles in the bank. I thought having a female in the room would help me, but no, her presence made me feel worse. You see, friend, I have always liked to think that we, women, should support each other no matter the consequences or our places in society—simply because we have a lot in common and can join forces to overcome obstacles and share joy in each other's achievements. I think there is a word for this—what is it, again? I think it's called "solidarity." That sort of unspoken support, but still something you can feel. I did that when I was in her shoes, interviewing college students. Wall Street can be intimidating sometimes; imagine when you are a young girl trying to make your way in. I immediately started battling with intrusive thoughts in my head: *What is up with this interview approach? Is there a stain on my suit? Do I not look okay? Are they trying to intimidate me? Show superiority? Did I say something wrong?* Not that I had said much that far in the interview. Quickly, I concluded that nothing good could come out of that interaction.

We proceeded with the questions. As I started answering, trying to make myself more comfortable and personable, I realized it wasn't working. So, I got more nervous instead. My voice started trembling. The words wouldn't come out. I could not focus.

I wasn't able to answer the one technical question they asked. The male interviewer looked into my eyes, still not mentioning my name, and impatiently proceeded to ask a sequence of two back-to-back questions without allowing me time to answer the first one. I felt rushed. I froze. Ouch, right? I thought I was failing in what felt like an interrogation type of interaction. With no time to answer the first question, he threw the second one right in—left me feeling like I had just gotten punched on each of my cheekbones. I started to blush, sweat, and shake my hands because I was overwhelmed. I realized I was going through an interrogation and not an internship interview. My body immediately told me: *Run, run, run.* Feeling like they were invading my emotional space, I asked myself: *Why is he taking this personally? Why is he choosing to talk to me without giving me a fair chance to answer his questions?* I am simply a college student looking for a summer internship.

Trembling and almost crying, still, with my cheeks burning and all sweaty, I said: "I truly appreciate your time. May I please leave the room? I thank you for your time." They excused me.

I left the building crying hysterically, my heart racing, and immediately called Noah. Still shaking and not being able to breathe, the dialogue went something like this:

Noah: "What's up? Why are you crying? Are you okay? What happened?"

Ladyane: "This is not for me. I do not think I am supposed to do this anymore. I can't keep doing this to myself. I am failing. I don't understand why it happened this way."

Noah: "What are you talking about?"

Ladyane: "The interview was terrible. It didn't even last 10 minutes. It wasn't an interview. It felt like an interrogation. It was a nightmare."

Noah: "I am so sorry, Buba (Read: Boo-bah) Sheli[1]. I am here for you. Drink some water. Where do you have to go now?"

Ladyane: "I am heading over to class."

Noah: "Let's meet later."

Ladyane: "Okay. I love you."

Noah: "I love you more."

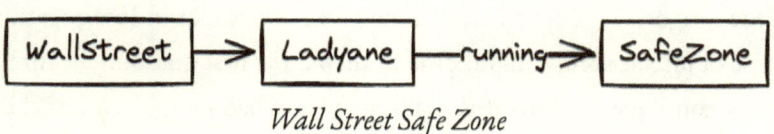

Wall Street Safe Zone

When I started my career and was on the other side of the table interviewing college students, I learned early on that one of the main questions we should ask a potential summer intern is, "Tell me about yourself." The answer to this question will direct the interview, and

---

1. Buba Sheli is a kind way to say "My doll" in Hebrew.

everything will flow as expected. Call it "Interviewing Summer Candidates for Dummies," if you will.

Two years later, I joined this same bank as an Associate. Yes, you are reading it right. All because of professional networking and hard work. What do they say again? What goes around, comes around. Indeed.

After the interrogation interview, I headed over to my college campus, went to the ladies' restroom, wiped my tears, tried to put myself together, and went to class trying to feel as if nothing happened, but I could not stop reliving those horrifying fifteen minutes that felt like long hours. I couldn't focus. Then it hit me: I was supposed to have one more round of interviews with one last bank, another one from the top five, and I thought to myself: I am not going to these interviews anymore.

Like a never-ending cycle, I did not allow myself enough time to process what happened. I started prepping for the last set of interviews with another top-five global bank. These interviews were my last chance. There was nothing left. Two days before my interview, I emailed my contact at the bank to say that I was excited about the interview and very much looking forward to the opportunity. I met him during a job fair on campus. He replied and said he was excited for me and looked forward to seeing me. I thought, *Ha ha, interesting*.

The Ideal Summer Internship Interview

This bank was the only one left that could give me a chance to stay in the United States. The first set of interviews happened on campus. In an attempt to avoid my bad luck from the previous horrifying interview, I woke up at 5:15 a.m. I thought that if I did things slightly differently from last time, I could change my situation and cast away any bad luck. We have to hang on to anything we have, right? Superstition it is, then! It was the only thing I had left other than preparing myself to do my best.

Having the interviews on campus helped. The environment was more relaxed. While my classmates and I were sitting outside the interview rooms waiting for our turns, we would cheer each other and change the conversation topic a bit to relax. We all knew we were nervous and purposefully attempted to change the subject to anything other than "Did you prepare?" "Did you read the latest in the financial news?" "Did you see this and that?" "What is a bond again?" That intentional attempt to distract ourselves helped me. The last student came out of the interview room. I knew they would call me to go in in a few minutes. I messaged Noah and said, *This is it. I am going in*. He replied, *You are a star. Remember that*.

With a warm smile on her face, the bank's HR campus representative, with whom I had interacted before, said: "Ladyane, your turn." With that "*You are a star*" mindset, I went in. As soon as I walked in, both interviewers were chatting with each other and laughing. The female interviewer said with a smile, "*Good morning, Ladyane. Have a seat, please.*" Do you know how powerful that simple sentence was to me? The female referred to me by my first name! She also had a smile on her face, and they both looked me in the eye. Not anywhere else. I immediately thought, "*I would love to work with these guys.*"

The male asked me, "How is your day going so far?" I said with a smile on my face: "Good. How about yours?" And he said sarcastically, "Ah, you know, living the dream." We all laughed, nodding in agreement. They started by asking me about college classes I liked and disliked. We moved on to the more personal questions, where I said I learned English in college. They looked impressed, and the female interviewer said: "Well, keep carrying on, Ladyane, your English is excellent." Do you see what I see, friend? These are supporting words. Encouraging words. They asked me about my Excel proficiency, to which William, the male interviewer, said: "Whatever you don't know, we will teach you." It felt as though I had the spot already. They knew their position enabled them to nurture and make the best of my ambition. It was a healthy exchange. They did not ask any technical questions. They finished the interview by thanking me for my time and saying the bank would be in touch. I thanked them with a massive smile on my face. I left the interview room and went on with my day.

A few days later, I received a call from the bank's HR campus representative saying I did great and was moving on to the Super Day. Super Day in the investment banking industry typically refers to the final round of summer internship interviews. During this final stage, students who have successfully passed the early rounds of interviews are invited into the office for a full day of intensive interviews and assessments. As soon as I hung up, I called Noah and said, "*I got into the next round.*" He laughed and said, "*I knew it!*"

A light lit up in my head, almost like an amazing idea had popped into my brain. I chose to block out that terrible interrogation-like interview and think about my last interview with the last bank. I went into manifestation mode—I created a mental vision board where I imagined myself interviewing and doing great. Little did I know back then that I had started exercising an emotional muscle that would be one of my tools to ride my emotional waves in the future.

The Power of Manifestation

When you manifest your desires and intentionally envision your actions, you actively pursue opportunities and gain clarity on your goals.

Friend, can we talk about the power of manifestation for a minute here? Manifestation starts with clarity of intention. How can we have clarity of intention if our daily lives are so busy? With all the roles we juggle daily and the countless tasks we face, how can we find a moment of clarity to understand what we truly desire in life when society imposes such unrealistic expectations on us as women? Well, the quick answer is that we don't have the time. And, in this scenario, most of us, at some point in our lives, are constantly chasing these unrealistic expectations instead of focusing on our true personal desires.

In general, today, we do much more than our grandmothers used to do, more than our moms used to do. Yet, the legacy of societal expectations imposed by generations ago still chases us. Friend, let me give you a few real-life examples: If a woman intentionally decides to pause her career to dedicate herself to her family, society is saying, "How come? Why are you doing this? Don't do this! How about your financial independence? What a terrible fate," finishing with "She is doomed." Another example is if a woman decides to be the breadwinner in her family, society says, "How did you let this happen? What about the husband? Shouldn't he be making money too? How come you make more money than he does? That's it—he will never work again." If a woman decides not to get married and have children of her own, society is saying, "Why are you doing this to yourself?" Or, "Poor thing, she hasn't been able to find a husband, so she will have the child alone." Lastly, if a woman decides not to get married and not have children, society says: "Your clock is ticking! Hey, when are you finding yourself someone? You aren't getting any younger." You see, friend, these questions and affirmations society tells us are just a projection of a belief system created generations ago that has never been challenged. Why does it need to be challenged? Because it's not sustainable for us!

Friend, my point about society's expectations and our power of manifestation is that it is challenging to intentionally manifest our desires when we are under constant pressure to deliver what society expects from us.

We know that having the intention and clarity to pursue what we genuinely want becomes challenging when we have several societal expectations imposed upon us. Social media today does not make it any easier. So, how can we manifest our desires organically? How can we create the time we already do not have? The expectations will never go away. But we can create opportunities to allow ourselves to have the time. This creation of opportunity is a habit; —it is a behavior pattern that needs to be practiced and nurtured. For example, during my college years, I manifested my desire to launch my career in the US by waking up early, meditating, and having a cup of coffee while I envisioned my day and what I could do to get closer to that goal. Note that I did not plan out how my day would be. I envisioned what I was going to achieve that particular day. There is a difference between the first and the latter; the first depends on others, while I control the latter. When you manifest your desires and intentionally envision your actions, you actively pursue opportunities and gain clarity on your goals. Allow yourself the time to do that; you deserve it. Ultimately, you start seeing opportunities when they aren't so obvious. The smallest habits yield greater outcomes. Soon enough, the flow is organic; it comes from within. You achieve your goals, and magic starts to happen. Do you remember I said it was going to be magical?

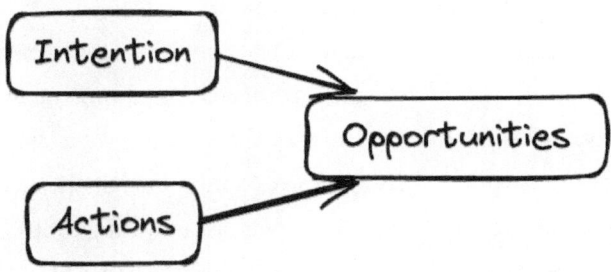

The Way to Create Opportunities

With this manifestation mindset, I went to sleep the night before my Super Day, thinking: "I have already accomplished so much. It cannot be that, on a day when I meet so many people, I will not be able to show them that I deserve a spot. I will try my best, and I will be myself. I got this. I will show them what I know and what I don't know. And, for what I do not know, I will make them believe I can learn." Friend, the power of your thoughts is incredible.

I woke up and checked my emails while sipping my cup of coffee. One of the emails was from my FWA mentor at 5 a.m., saying, "You got this, Ladyane." It felt so good to read that from one of my role models. I got dressed—I had selected the interview outfit the night before, so there were no surprises on the wardrobe front. Minimizing risk, is what they say.

Leaving my home and commuting to the financial district in downtown NYC, I thought of nothing. I felt like I was in a parallel reality. One part of me could not believe I had gotten that far—making my way to an investment bank's Super Day. I could almost touch the achievement with my bare hands. In the crowded train heading over to the NYC financial district, I manifested my day in my head; I thought of all the knowledge I wanted to share with my interviewers, how I wanted to talk to them, and how I wanted them to perceive me. I wanted to do everything I could so that they could see me for who I indeed was; a hard-working young girl from Brazil who was accomplished academically, and could attain much more for them.

Shortly after I arrived, the first half of the day began. There were a total of about four to five rounds of interviews—Some of them with one person, others with two. Pause for lunch. All over again, but in a group setting this time. HR grouped us into smaller teams of about five to six candidates and placed each team in a meeting room. The HR representative presented us in the meeting room with a BCP (Business Continuity Planning) problem that impacted the bank's daily operations. The interviewers sat in the chairs by the meeting room walls, allowing us to take the spotlight as the "executives" for the day.

As soon as I got into the meeting room, I saw William, the male executive who had interviewed me on campus. We made eye contact but did not speak. I quickly realized he was there as an interviewer, observing and taking notes. As we started deliberating the BCP problem, the challenges, and the potential solutions, I would quickly look at William, hoping to get some "You got this!" type of look. But no—he looked different. Maybe even intimidating—he had a poker face. That did not help me, but I eventually realized my focus was not on how reassuring the eye contact from my future manager could be but how well I could handle the team-setting interview. I quickly realized they did not expect us to find a solution to the BCP problem but wanted to see how well we managed the situation. So, I purposefully reassured the other team's comments and added other options as possibilities. I included numbers and added a game plan option. I had a voice. I was very aware that my accent was super strong; I was so nervous, how could it not be strong? But I did not stop. Soon enough, it was all over. We wrapped it up. They gave us some goodies. Thanked us for our time and set us free. I was done and feeling good. On the main floor, a group of us started chatting, and despite my terrible tension headache, I decided to join the group and grab some drinks at a bar nearby.

Three weeks passed, and I was still waiting for a call from the bank's HR representative. I decided to follow up with an email: *Have you made a decision already? If not, do you know when you expect to make one?* The HR representative replied almost immediately, *We haven't, but we plan on making a final decision by the end of the week, and we will be in touch.* I liked that answer, it meant that I still had a chance. While one side of me was thinking: *Forget about it! Why do you do this to yourself? Just move on. You will not get it*, the other one shouted, *It worked out. Do not worry. This opportunity is meant to be.* Which version of Ladyane should I have listened to? Again, remember the expectation versus reality battle? It took me some time to understand my new reality was finally manifesting before my eyes.

After the email from the HR representative, I took my phone off mute and set it with the highest ringtone possible—I did not want to miss her call.

The Call

It was a rainy spring Thursday afternoon. A few days have passed since the bank's HR representative emailed me. I am at work and still sharing the same office with my manager. My phone rings, and it's the bank's HR representative's phone number. I excuse myself and step outside to take the phone call in private. I always liked to pick up the phone by saying my name; I thought it sounded professional. So I picked up the phone:

"This is Ladyane."

The bank's HR representative was always kind and professional. She eased me into the conversation, a gift in such a stressful situation. She said something like, "Ladyane, congratulations! You did very well, and we would like to extend an offer for you to spend the summer with us. Would you like to join us?" I just couldn't believe it. Again, for a few seconds, I was not there. I was in that train-ride parallel reality. It was as if that reality was pulling me in and screaming its lungs out: *Enough of this nonsense! THIS IS YOU NOW, LADYANE! YOU DESERVE THIS! Grab it! This belongs to you, and you belong to this new reality!* After enduring ten seconds of silence, punctuated by my inner screams, I responded to her with laughter, saying, "Absolutely!" She started laughing too and said: "That's great news! Please be on the lookout for our official offer in your email. Later on, you will receive another email where we will tell you everything about the team you will be joining and your manager. Congratulations, Ladyane. We are excited to have you here during this summer." I thanked her, and we hung up.

I immediately called Noah, my sister, and my mom in Brazil to deliver the big news. They were all thrilled. I returned to my shared office and told my manager, who cried and hugged me. "Ladyane, I am so proud of you. You deserve this." I went on with my day, unable to focus. I was in shock. Later that day, while celebrating with Noah, I realized that the power of manifestation, combined with hard work and determination, eventually led to something magical happening.

The bank's placement email came in a few weeks later. Again, everything was aligned. I was assigned to join William's team—the same William who interviewed me in the first round of interviews and was part of the group interview during the Super Day.

I could breathe again.

I could finally stop running from the rock rolling downhill chasing me.

I had finally found myself in my safety zone.

But only for a short time.

Along with the feelings of excitement and accomplishment, I felt scared. I had doubts. For the first time since I embarked on my new US life, I feared losing something I had worked so hard to achieve, something that would eventually add more labels to *Ladyane* (this time, the new label was *Wall Street Vice President*).

Friend, you have seen it—fear was never foreign to me. But this time was different. Before, I feared not being able to do something. This time, I feared I would lose something I had tried so hard to accomplish, and that was everything to me. Do you see the difference? Labels are tricky, right? If we aren't careful, they can hurt us. They can own us and make us carry much heavier mental and emotional weight than we're able. I eventually found the balance of carrying all the labels on my shoulder because I learned labels are not meant to be mentally detrimental.

On the contrary, I learned to benefit from these labels and use them for personal growth. However, the fear was present and projected in spiral thoughts that made me doubt my ability to succeed in such a fast-paced industry. Unknown to me at that moment, I started showing my first signs of high-functioning anxiety, the typical thought pattern of *This is too good to be true*.

I did not give much attention to those thoughts back then. Think of it this way: I saved them in a little mental compartment and decided to deal with them later. I did not put a time stamp on it, I carried on and avoided dealing with these feelings. Instead, I focused on the task at hand. I focused on launching my career through that summer internship. In my mind, I manifested a promising career and financial stability, all I wanted and cared about back then. Nothing else mattered. So, once again, I did not ride that emotional wave; I chose to put the feelings and doubts in a little mental compartment to deal with them later. I neglected them. I did it because I prioritized something else—the financial stability, keeping my immigration status, the stability I so much craved for. My purpose was to achieve the so-wished stability I lacked when I arrived in the US. I wanted to change my narrative; this change was my purpose then.

On the first day of my summer internship, I embraced the conviction that launching my career in that bank was my destined path. I convinced myself that working at that bank, with those people, in that environment, was what I was meant to do. I ultimately and once again adapted, camouflaged, and blended in, just like I did when I was a child, moving from small towns to big cities, from one school to another—just like I did when I first arrived in the US.

Here is my routine as a summer analyst in a top global investment bank: I was the first in my team to arrive at the office and the last to leave. I worked long hours; I always delivered more than they asked for. I networked with everyone, everywhere. I worked some more. I had some scattered happy-hour hangovers here and there—they say, "Work hard, play hard," right? I think they mean that, literally. I went on multiple lunch meetings and coffee breaks. I asked for specific feedback during my one-on-one meetings with my manager. I also met with my manager's manager (in corporate, we call it "Skip level") several times. I shadowed team members. I was like a sponge—absorbing everything from everyone.

The full-time job offer at the end of my summer internship was the official stamp of my career launch. Upon my college graduation, I started my Wall Street journey. What typically requires eight to ten years of consistent dedication, I achieved in a mere six years—fueled by relentless hard work, unyielding determination, and always accompanied by my ever-growing supporting village. After all, it is impossible to achieve life milestones alone.

So, friend, let's pause a bit. Could I ask you to do something? If you feel alone in your journey at this moment or do not have enough people in your supporting village, please put my book down (I won't take it personally, I promise) and go out there and try connecting with people. You see, don't just meet people. Connect with them. There is a difference. First, you keep adding more followers on social media and your contact list, nothing more. The latter, you enable an exchange of thoughts and engage in a bond encompassing various aspects of life, bridging the personal and the professional; this is an art nowadays. The first is about quantity. The latter is about quality. I promise you this effort will yield something back to you. We do not get anywhere alone. I did not get to sit here and write this book alone. I did not become a Wall Street Vice President, six years out of college, alone. There was, and there still is, a gigantic supporting village beside me, holding my hand through my journey. I would like for you to have your village, too. What do you think?

Chapter 5

THE ABUNDANCE PHASE BEGINS

I am talking about mindset—our actions and thoughts shape the outcome of our lives.

THE ABUNDANCE PHASE BEGAN when I entered my senior year in college. And by the abundance phase, I am not talking about financial abundance only. I am talking about mindset; our actions and thoughts shape the outcome of our lives. I kept envisioning graduating with honors, so I worked for it. I kept focusing on launching a promising career, so I did it. I persisted in exploring the endless options for achieving and maintaining financial stability, so I did it. I focused on creating a professional supporting village, so I did it. Friend, I am simply referring to having your motivations crystal clear and combining them with a consistent and persistent dedicated effort to achieve something more significant, to achieve what you genuinely desire. There is nothing else besides this mindset and consistent dedication to the endeavor.

During my last academic year, I received two academic excellence-based awards (it felt like I was getting paid to study) and had a full-time job at a top global investment bank waiting for me upon graduation, along with the assurance of a job visa. Who would have thought that the little seven-year-old girl, losing her father to a terrible disease, would eventually be in New York City living her best life? At that moment, that was the life I wanted. That was the life I loved. That was the life that I created for myself.

We can achieve beautiful things when we set a goal,
manifest our motivations, and set a trajectory. We
shall not worry about the pace. We shall envision the
journey and stay the course.

With my primary concerns, the full-time job and visa addressed, I embraced my academic mentor's counsel and began crafting a senior honors thesis in Political Science. I saw the process as an opportunity to delve deeply into a topic of my interest, engage in extensive research and critical analysis, and work closely with my mentor, benefiting from her expertise and insights. All these aspects made this opportunity too compelling to resist. Not to mention the academic recognition that came with graduating with honors—it's a big deal. There is something I have always found admirable about the writing process. And so, that's what I tried to do; I enriched my life by crafting a ninety-three-page senior honors thesis. And today, I humbly hope I can, on some level, enrich your life by sharing some of my journey with you in this book.

She Will Be The Heart & Soul of Her People

She created her safety zone where she belonged.

It is now May 2012, and the FWA-Baruch mentorship program has just awarded me the Student of the Year honoree title as a recognition of my academic and professional achievements. They asked me to write and deliver the speech on that beautiful spring evening, the one I started this book with. Thankfully, the FWA hired a speech coach to assist me with my speech delivery; I do not believe I could have delivered the speech so confidently if it wasn't for what my speech coach once told me in one of our rehearsal meetings. One day, witnessing my failed attempts to hide my accent while practicing my speech, my speech coach candidly said: "Ladyane, please, do not try to hide your accent. It is part of who you are. It is your identity. It is this speech's identity. And, it's beautiful." Words of affirmation are powerful, am I right? I will never forget how powerful her words were to me. These words echoed in my brain countless times in several circumstances when I doubted my ability to be understood – every time I sat in meeting rooms full of senior executives, and every time I led calls full of experienced professionals and industry regulators. My accent is beautiful.

And this is how I concluded the first part of my transformation. Up on that stage, on that beautiful spring evening, Ladyane was no longer that little girl from Brazil. All the experiences, lessons, and waves I have ridden up to that point in my life led me to go up on that stage and tell everyone confidently: "This is who I was; this is who I am today. And here is how I will be in the future. It is promising. Wait and see. I could feel the safety in having the ability to choose the changes in my life. I could feel the fulfillment of embracing these changes and committing to them. Up on that stage I could finally feel what it was like to make decisions out of options and not necessities.

Ladyane stood on that stage, transformed into a confident young Latina, ready to launch her promising Wall Street career and graduate with honors. But, above all, there was simply Ladyane: a young girl who was no longer afraid of not having opportunities, a young girl who did not have to keep moving from place to place to find her safety zone. She created her safety zone where she belonged. She learned and transformed.

Transformation is a journey, not a destination. If you feel it's over, then something vital is missing. We are meant to keep learning, exploring, and evolving.

And because transformation never ends, I went seeking more. Noah and I decided to live together and I used that to overcome a big fear I realized I had: I did not see myself ever getting married. I was afraid of being married. Today, I understand that the unstable family dynamic I witnessed growing up, where marriage was predominantly vulnerable and doomed with infidelity and emotional abuse, caused this fear. I saw myself as a mother, though. Tricky but not impossible—we, women, can do it all, right? And I think I saw myself being a mother simply because my mother was amazing; she did it all alone while having an immense village of family and close friends. So, one day, I told Noah: "I do not see myself getting married. But I see myself having children." Noah took that as an opportunity to show me that a stable marriage is possible. He was on a mission to prove a point—so we moved in together. With the positive experiences, I eventually felt safe and realized we could have a safe marriage together. Noah and I have been creating and transforming our lives together for seventeen years.

So, a few years after I launched my Wall Street
career, I started the most rewarding and important
role in my life: I became a mother. I became the heart
and soul of my children.

As if launching my career in Wall Street wasn't challenging enough, I decided to shake things up even more by diving headfirst into a new chapter, a life-changing endeavor. I decided to embrace Judaism. You may be asking, why? Didn't you have enough on your plate? Yes! That's precisely one of the reasons that led me to want to explore Judaism. You see, friend, I will not tell you, "Do it, it's great!" or "I highly recommend it." No, this is an extremely personal choice. It involved some deep soul-searching and deep questioning of who I was and who I wanted to become. Remember I said we are constantly evolving? That's what it is; if I do not feel that I am continually "becoming," then I think something is off. And it is not because I did not feel I belonged, on the contrary, during our daily lives, experiencing Judaism with Noah, his relatives, parents, and friends, I found as though I had belonged forever. I felt I did not have to change my essence to feel that I belonged. I felt as though I had finally found the connection I was missing up to that point in my life. And so I took on a two-year long learning journey with my rabbi.

On a sunny August day in 2014, accompanied by part of my support-ing village, my rabbi, my mother, my mother-in-law, and Noah's aunt, I stood before the Beit Din (Jewish Court), where we talked about my beliefs, my learnings, and how I was going to ensure the continuity of Judaism. They thanked me for my time, said I did a wonderful job, and welcomed me to the Jewish community. Saying my Jewish name, *Ariela*, they led me to my mikveh—a ritual of bath immersion that symbolizes spiritual purification and renewal and officializes the conversion process. Why did I change my name? I did not change my name. When one becomes Jewish by choice, they are tasked to choose a Jewish name. After so much research and brainstorming with my rabbi, I decided to follow the Gematria approach, which has a blessing associated with a name and a numeric value for each of the letters in the name. Gematria is a method of interpreting Hebrew words and phrases using numeral values. It is predominantly used in Kaballah, where numeral values are often seen as symbolic and meaningful beyond their literal significance.

Ariela means the "Lioness of God," the heart of her generation. The blessing associated with the name Ariela is: *Her life will be one of song and cheer. She will be the heart and soul of her people.*

In my case, my family is my people. So, a few years after I launched my Wall Street career, I started the most rewarding and important role in my life: I became a mother. I became the heart and soul of my children.

Chapter 6

LADYANE LIMA, WHERE ARE YOU? PART II

Financial stability manifested in various ways for me, and I embraced it fully.

I N 2018, I WAS a Vice President in the Compliance department at one of the top five global investment banks. Financial stability manifested in various ways for me, and I embraced it fully. Before turning thirty, I bought my first home in the New Jersey suburbs, securing a great education for my children. I enjoyed the freedom to own two cars, take spontaneous trips, and fully invest in my 401(k) while putting my hard-earned money to work. I supported my family and felt I was living the American dream. But while I appreciated the financial stability and progress in my career, there were moments that left me wondering if it was time to pause and redefine what the American dream truly meant to me.

What's coming up for you, Ladyane?
Try to go back.
Reverse your trajectory.
Stay true to yourself.
Remember why you are here.
Remember who Ladyane is.
Where are you, Ladyane Lima? Come back.

I am in this small office. Even though our office building faced the Hudson River, my team and I didn't get the luxury of a river view—we were stuck on the 'scenic' side facing away from it. Today, I think I would not have let my emotions take over during that particular meeting if I had been facing the river. I always thought that staring at the water was calming. Maybe if I had looked at the river while hearing my work colleague's perspective on me, I would have calmed down. Who knows? It happened. It's in the past. But I will share it with you because that meeting was a turning point for me. After this meeting, combined with other moments I had been presented with since I became a mother trying to juggle a Wall Street career, I decided it was time to change.

My work colleague sits across from me and shares his perspective on a work-related situation he did not quite like. He sounds frustrated. But I honestly do not remember much of the meeting because I blocked it from my memory.

Since our manager was working from home that day, we could quickly use his office to chat. Why did we need to chat? The context is quite simple. I had just recently returned from maternity leave. However, my manager moved me to a different business function and told me about it the day I returned from maternity leave. As I recall, I believe there was a reorganizational change, and it made sense for me to move to this new function. It was a different business function, so I needed to learn all about it immediately upon my return from maternity leave. I didn't like the change because the business function was very different from my previous one, and they needed me to provide coverage on certain weekends. At the time, I had two young children, so I was frustrated about being excluded from the decision-making process for a role that would affect my personal life and my ability to be a present mother on weekends. In retrospect, what frustrated me most was not being consulted about the change in my role. I felt as though I had no control over my own career.

I was tasked with learning the new business function. What that means is "hands-on learning." You learn as you perform the work, which can be stressful. So I learned. Fast. Soon enough, I reviewed other colleagues' work, and, like anywhere else, I would catch inconsistencies. It happens; we always miss something. That's why we have people reviewing work. Some executives used to say I was a "sweet talker." They argued I was good at delivering feedback and bad news. So I was assigned some reviewer responsibilities, requiring me to review my colleague's work—the one I needed to have the meeting with. It turned out he didn't quite like receiving feedback from me. I do not recall the exact words exchanged during the meeting—again, I blocked it from my memory. I remember bits and pieces like when he harshly said "How come you did not have to interview for the role?" And something along the lines of me being difficult and overstepping my role followed by our manager should review his work, not me.

There I was. I was desperately trying to remember why I was in that room at that moment. *I worked hard to be here. Wait. But I did not want to be here. Not in this room. Not with this person. I did not ask to be placed in that function. Stay true to yourself, Ladyane. Breathe.*

To say I felt uncomfortable is an understatement. I was confused. I was perplexed. I did not know what to say or what to do. I remember talking to myself, trying to think of a way out of what felt like a hostile conversation where my coworker was the only one speaking—a monologue. He did not notice anything because he kept talking as if I was paying attention and listening. He lacked self-awareness, and I do not think he realized he was the only one talking. But it was advantageous for me. I guess?

I focused on breathing and trying everything not to blush —I simply let him talk. It was the only thing I could do at that moment. I wanted to run.

When he finished sharing his perspective on how I should perform my role and what he thought of me, I gave him a subtle smile and said: "I'm sorry you felt this way. We will figure something out." I desperately needed a way out of that room, so I said whatever would get me out of that disturbing exchange the fastest. I fled.

Let's pause here, friend. Let's recap. I felt like a boundary had just been crossed — a coworker had no full context of my career trajectory, providing me with a distorted view of my role, in a meeting room and I was the one apologizing at the end. It was a good moment for me to reflect on how to learn to set boundaries in the workplace.

I calmly placed my notebook on my desk and walked to the ladies' room. I cried compulsively but quietly. I did not want anyone to hear me—It was the first and last time I cried because of work. I grabbed a cup of water from the pantry and went into an empty meeting room to call Noah. Despite my failed attempt to describe to Noah what happened, I remember him saying: "Whatever you need, Buba. Can you come home?" I thought the meeting room walls could hear me for some reason, and I felt ashamed. I was afraid. I honestly don't remember much, but I recalled I said something disturbing happened but that I was okay.

I returned to my office desk and could not focus for the rest of the day. Luckily, I had just a few hours before I could bid farewell to that horrifying workday without too many dirty looks. I felt that some of my coworkers resented me because I did not have to interview for the new role and could work from home two days a week. The flexible arrangement was an agreement William and I had when he asked me to join him back at the bank 2 years earlier. I did not need to interview for that new role because, during my maternity leave absence, they cut me out of the previous function and placed me in this new one. So, people just gave me the dirty looks right and left without the full context.

I cried more that night, resting my head on Noah's lap.

That night, I realized I had long been in an abusive relationship with my career.

It was hard to fall asleep. I tossed and turned until exhaustion found me. In addition to having to deal with this experience, I was still handling the emotional wave of deciding to abruptly stop breastfeeding my son, which I will forever regret. Breastfeeding him made me feel whole. Love and connection are abundant between a mother and her child. However, every time I would return from my pumping and thirty-minute lunch break (I would eat lunch while pumping breastmilk), I would get dirty looks from some coworkers. I did not know how to set boundaries back then. I will tell you more about boundaries soon. Today, I would probably put on everyone's calendar *"Milk Pumping Time—Do Not Disturb"* (A diplomatic way of saying "back off"). I did not know any better back then. So, I deliberately stopped my incredible and personal journey prematurely, and that caused me emotional and physical pain.

The meeting and all the emotional load I was carrying for a while led me to surrender. I succumbed to the pressure of the workload, to the abrupt change in working schedule, to the stress of being asked to provide weekend coverage for the team, to the inability to keep my working-from-home arrangement, to the pressure of handling some dirty looks when I returned from the pumping room during my lunch break, and to the lack of control over my career. It was all too much to handle. It got way too personal. I was getting sick. And I surrendered.

The Art of Surrendering

What feeds my soul?

Surrendering to your emotions and understanding yourself opens up a whole new world of possibilities that may not necessarily fit with other's expectations of you, but it fits your expectations of yourself. And that, friend, is empowering.

Up to that point in my life, I was in a different type of mode. I was programmed to get things done and disregard what my body told me. I just kept going. I kept hustling and thinking, *I will not return to Brazil. I will never struggle financially again. I will help my family.* In a way, that unpleasant meeting was my key to opening my new world of possibilities. I am forever grateful for it.

I Learned How to Ride My Emotional Waves

Steady. Strong. Vigilant.

The following day, I woke up feeling like I had a hangover. In all, I must have gotten four hours of restless sleep. I started writing in my journal in an attempt to ride that overwhelming emotional wave so that I could feel a bit more prepared to have another day at work. My therapist had encouraged me always to write to manage my anxiety. At that point, I had been going to therapy for about four years. My therapist argued that writing was a sort of cleansing tool—flushing everything out of my being so that I could make space for more being. So I wrote. That day, I finished the journal entry with the following: *Writing is about transformation.* Followed by my mantra: *Steady. Strong. and Vigilant.*

Friend, do you have a mantra? A mantra is a powerful tool. It allows you to affirm yourself and your purpose. Above all, it helps you in difficult times. Magic does not happen out of thin air, friend. It's not easy, but with the right tools, magic happens. Create a mantra that aligns with what you aim for on a high-level, that bigger picture—ask yourself, what do these words bring up to me? Stop. Reflect. Be present. Breathe. Write. Repeat. I will give you my mantra as an example: By *Steady*, I mean that I shall be consistent with the transformation process. I shall be steadily consistent with the commitment to evolve—to the commitment of just "being." By *Strong*, I mean that I shall be resilient and have a firm conviction of my purpose; by *Vigilant*, I mean that I shall watch and be attentive to the world around me and my intuition. I shall always be aware and attuned.

Think about your mantra—I assure you that having one will pay off.

On my train ride to the office that morning, I realized I needed to re-create my safety zone again. I needed to evolve once again. I needed to transform. But, you may be thinking, *Why so radical? Why transform again? You have worked so hard to be where you are.* My ambition to become a Vice President at a top global investment bank overtook me. It blurred my ability to think or plan anything else differently. It stopped me from seeing the potential red flags that my career was showing me, especially after motherhood. I realized that besides having reasonable monetary compensation, being a Vice President gave me nothing else. It started creating a hole in my soul. Before getting promoted to Vice President, I craved that success so intensely that I often closed my eyes to the warning signs and ignored red flags, simply fueled by the ambition to achieve the wished Vice President title. On that train ride, I realized my transformation was happening way before becoming Vice President. My version of the American dream changed.

I will forever be grateful for the lessons, connections, experiences, and financial stability I achieved due to a stable Wall Street career. It is fruitful and can be a stepping stone to achieve great things. Due to this career, I can afford to stay home today and be emotionally present and fully available to my children—I would do it all over again despite the tears of joy and sadness. Remember, it is not easy, but it *is* magical. So, friend, if you are going through that phase and asking yourself if it is all worth it. Pause. Breathe. Write. We make sacrifices, but there is a reward waiting for us in the end.

The purpose was to be a cycle breaker.

I would go through that meeting again. I would work long and late hours again. I would be exhausted again. I would do it all over again simply because I now know that the purpose was not to become a Vice President after all. The purpose was to be a cycle breaker. The purpose was to change the course of my life and of those I love dearly. The purpose was to ensure my family and I would never struggle financially again. The purpose was to be the safety-zone enabler. I accomplished that. So I concluded I was ready to move on. And cheers to more labels—Enabler of Safety Zone? Check; Former Wall Street Vice President, Check; Cycle breaker? Check!

That year, I started bidding farewell to Wall Street slowly, steadily, strongly, and vigilantly. But before I tell you how it happened, I wanted to share with you the journey of having a Wall Street career, being a mother, and adding a worldwide pandemic to the mix.

The Supporting Village & Career

Earning a spot on the list of 'go-to' individuals for getting the job done requires significant dedication and commitment.

I had a fantastic manager during my first year as an analyst at the bank that recruited me from college (Bank 1). The Bank was amazing and supportive of first-year analysts like myself. I was also paired with a mentor. As a first-year Analyst, I was overseeing and managing risk associated with Corporate Actions. Sounds fun, right? It was! The part I liked the most was my one-on-ones with my manager and my mentor. My role was simple yet meaningful; I was supposed to research, analyze, and create presentations associated with the operational risks for the deals for the week. Because of this presentation, the head of the department asked me to be an attendant at the weekly management meeting. There I was, two to three months into my new role, newly graduated from college, having to speak in front of experienced and well-spoken Wall Street executives. Other than me, there was also a female Vice President from whom I learned a lot.

My first meeting was okay. I was very nervous. It was the first time I was speaking in a room full of managers staring at me and asking questions. Before the first meeting, my manager at the time pulled me into a room and said: "Talk to me as if you are in that room." I stared at him and went into "game" mode. He then asked questions about the deals as if we were in that room. At the end, he says: "You did well, Ladyane. Go back and dig a bit deeper into the risk points I mentioned. Above all, it sounds like you know it all. Perception is reality, Ladyane."

Perception is reality. How powerful is that? My first manager on Wall Street soon became my role model. From that day on, I worked on sounding confident about my work. I would speak up during meetings as if I were one of them, and they treated me as such. Soon enough, these same managers would trust my opinion and rely on my insights about the several risks associated with the deals.

To make things a bit more interesting, that year, Hurricane Sandy happened, and I was in charge of ensuring top managers and critical team members would have a way to work despite not having power or access to computers—does that sound like that BCP (Business Continuity Planning) group interview assignment? The financial district's NYC office was underwater—my office building lost power, people lost power, and homes flooded. Despite these challenges, I quickly contacted over twenty team members during the hurricane and devised a plan to ensure the business function would operate the next day. Clients needed payment, shares required moving, and we had to take action. The next morning, I joined a call with the global head of the department, the local head of the department, and my manager. In the call, I was asked to speak about where we were and how we would move forward, provided we had no ETA for when the physical office would be up and running. I worked all night long to ensure I would have a plan. After that meeting, my manager called me and said: "That was excellent stuff, Ladyane. Amazing bad news delivery." He and I laughed almost as if "Phew." After this experience, I became the go-to person when the topic was risk for corporate action and delivering bad news. I focused on learning and carrying on.

When I joined the bank that recruited me from college, William was bidding farewell to join another top global investment bank (Bank 2). I went to his farewell drinks, and we talked about what was next, the challenges, and how he was living the dream. A few months after Hurricane Sandy, William called me and said: "Do you want to join me here?"

Recap: I worked for William during my summer internship at Bank 1. A year and a half later, he joined another bank (Bank 2) and called me to see if he could bring me in as an associate. I was a first-year analyst, and to become an associate would have taken me two more years. Given that William was the one reaching out, I negotiated the terms of the transition from Bank 1 to Bank 2.

Once I had the official offer from Bank 2 with the hiring terms, I met with my manager because I wanted him to see that I appreciated him, the bank, and everything I had learned. I wanted them to see that I could return one day under the right terms for me but that, for now, the other bank's offer was impossible to refuse. No hard feelings. My manager was happy for me. Everyone was. I gave my resignation notice. Two weeks later, we gathered for my farewell drinks to celebrate Ladyane's swift promotion to associate at another prestigious global investment bank.

Let's pause for a bit, friend. Do you see how having a supporting village in your career is so important? Having a professional sponsor can open multiple doors. Having a mentor helps you explore possibilities when the doors open. I will tell you how. When William asked me if I wanted to join him in Bank 2, I immediately thanked him. I said I would consider it, and we could chat in a few days. Friend, when someone wants your work, never immediately offer an answer. Sit on it. I talked to my mentor a few times, and we explored a few options to negotiate. I started with the most aggressive one when William and I talked a few days later. We eventually settled on the following aspects: a higher title and salary and work-from-home arrangement. How was I able to negotiate? I did it because of the quality of my work and professional sponsorship.

My name came up somehow, somewhere for the role William called me about. The funny part is that this is the same bank that caused me my first panic attack when I was interviewing for a summer internship in college. I forgot all about that. I cared about the excellent, big, chunky salary and the title. The working-from-home arrangement was a bonus. William gave me everything I asked for. Everything worked out.

Almost two years into the job, I got a call. This executive I had worked with at the Bank 1 that hired me from college said she had joined this new team and needed help implementing new processes and leading new initiatives. She asked if I was interested. Three days later, I had coffee with her. The next day, I went back to the office and chatted with William about the pros and cons of potentially returning to Bank 1. I will only get into a few details about the decision-making process, but ultimately, it boiled down to more money, the same title, and more organizational stability. Again, another sponsor who had an open role and thought, "Ladyane can do it. Let me give her a call." Earning a spot on the list of go-to individuals for getting the job done requires significant dedication and commitment.

The transition from one bank to another was easy. It was almost as if they were both my homes. I realized I was finally building a professional reputation and liked it. I liked the recognition of my commitment. I liked the experience, and I wanted to feel productive. Noah and I had been married for almost three years and started planning the next steps—we were ready to buy our first home and have our first baby. I was excited about my career and living my version of the American dream. However, with such a fast-paced career, I started noticing some symptoms of high-functioning anxiety. Picture this: On the outside, I was competent, extremely productive, and all put together, but on the inside, I was worrying, had doubts, and couldn't relax. So I dived deep into guided meditation practice and journaling. My goal was to bring the pressure a notch down and take care of my mental well-being to prepare myself to become a mother.

Chapter 7

THE HEART & SOUL OF HER PEOPLE

*Motherhood is bidding farewell to your original self
and celebrating your reinvention.*

J OURNALING HAS ALWAYS BEEN opening doors for me. The process
of writing my feelings and my daily life in a safe and judgment-free
space is empowering. There is something about the process of journaling
that allows you to reflect on the truths you avoid and the truths you embrace, and with that comes self-awareness and personal growth. Let's face
it, we all have truths in our lives that we, purposefully or unconsciously,
try to ignore—the old and easy "save for later." But how long can we
sustain that? And, at what point do we open that "save for later" tab and
finally deal with the truth we have so long forgotten? There is something
liberating about writing "unpleasant" truths on a safe and judgment-free
piece of paper. We commit to our truth. We commit to face that the

truth may hurt, but that it still exists and is real and meaningful. There is so much personal growth in that. Here is a piece my personal growth journal excerpt:

February 11, 2015

My mother-in-law just visited from Israel to be with me for my planned surgery. We talked about a lot, which was quite interesting given that we were not fluent in each other's languages. However, I concluded that meeting my mother-in-law was meant to be and became part of my growth journey. My mother-in-law sounds almost like a little witch. And I love it. During this chat, she introduced me to something called "Life Alignment." We discussed my feelings and how I should align my feelings with myself. We talked about how anxious I have been and how I could handle this moving forward. We discussed why this is important—we agreed that I need this alignment to achieve what I want in life. I told her I felt like I had accomplished so many things career-wise, but now I want to become a mother. I told her I think I am mentally ready but lack the psychological strength because of my anxiety and stress. She told me every day is an opportunity to realign.

I bought the "Self Alignment" book that my mother-in-law and I discussed. It arrived the day she flew back to Israel after spending a few days with me to ensure my speedy recovery from my surgery. I felt loved. I felt I had a second mother who had embraced me for who I am—nothing else to fix or change. I felt thankful and excited.

Unpleasant truth—when it comes to meaningful life endeavors, there is no such thing as feeling "I am super ready!" followed by "I so got this!" No. I am a mother of three children today. I have been doing this for nine years and still do not believe I got it. I refuse to pretend I do. It's too exhausting and fake. It does not feel organic. So, I embrace my unpleasant truth. I embrace imperfection. What type of mother would I be if I were always perfect? What role model is the one that is perceived by her children as always put together and flawless? Does this exist? Can you show me, please? I am curious to know how being perfect at all times can be done. But, friend, I don't want to aim for perfection here. My children know me for who I am. And I am not perfect. Nor do I expect perfection from them. Period.

Friend, do you know what makes me feel at peace today with motherhood? It is the simple fact that I am not aiming for perfection. I aim to become a role model, to model imperfections and how I handle them. I am aiming to transform myself for the greater purpose of raising good human beings. I am far from a perfect mom. My kids joke around saying that I forget things—I have multiple ways to remind me of events, doctor appointments, playdates, etc. Noah and I have weekly family meetings to keep track of everything. We keep different color-coded calendars—life is more beautiful if colorful. Still, I forget things from time to time. Everyone knows I am not perfect, meaning I do not expect perfection from them. I feel I could have done something better in plenty of moments. However, the beautiful thing about loving and being loved is that you always get a chance to re-do something for as long as you are true to yourself and those who love you. You will get a second chance at some point, in an unexpected moment, or in the most unexpected circumstance.

There was no more considerable personal transformation for me than being a mother for the first time while managing a Wall Street career. I would do it again in a heartbeat because it is simply about the journey and the lessons I have learned. It is not about the destination, although I wouldn't want to live any other life than the one I have today. Transitioning into motherhood for the first time was the most transformative and overwhelming experience I have ever encountered. However, I quickly learned that motherhood fit me — I quickly embraced the change and committed to it with all imperfections, challenges, and lessons learned.

Juliette, my oldest daughter, was born on a beautiful November day in 2015. The most beautiful thirty-two hours of my life, filled with adrenaline and love. I immediately held her, crying tears of joy. There was no pain. There was no discomfort. I went into labor watching the movie *Inside Out* on a Sunday night and progressed to give birth on the following Monday at 8 p.m. While I held her and fed her, Noah and I kept crying and saying repeatedly, "We love you so much, Juliette." How crazy is it that you are so deeply in love with that little person you have just met? As soon as she was born, we looked at each other, full of tears of joy, and I said: "Hello, Juliette, it is so wonderful to meet you." In Portuguese, I added, "Mommy and Daddy love you so much, our light."

The first few days were insane. I felt everything and some more. The sleep deprivation and motherhood uncertainty shook me up. I was the first of my friends to become a mother, so I did not quite have a "supporting village" in that regard. I did not know many moms I could turn to. Social media was not my thing back then (one could argue it still isn't today), so I did not go out there seeking guidance other than from our pediatrician and my mother. I aimed to get to know Juliette, observe her, and love her. I did not worry about work. Work was secondary for me. I truly felt I had fulfilled my purpose; I felt happiness and fulfillment from within. I woke up excited and thankful that Juliette had made me become another version of myself, which I had never seen before, but I was excitedly surprised to meet my new self.

I could not think of a better introduction to motherhood than the one Juliette gave me. I like to say that each of my children has a purpose in my life—Juliette is my emotional compass. Don't worry; I do not seek emotional coaching from a young child. But Juliette is unique. She is witty and outspoken. There is no emotion Juliette feels that is not out there; one way or the other, this girl is true to herself and is not afraid. She speaks her mind. And I love it! I won't take credit for it, though, I think this is how she is. Maybe she gets a bit from me—I confess I tend to speak my mind. But then, Juliette has formed opinions about several topics. That is all on her. She is well-articulated and good at organizing her thoughts. It is like she allows us to enter her world and tune in emotionally. Juliette is nine years old, loves art, is an actress, and a swimmer. She channels her intensity into acting, and she loves it. It is beautiful to watch.

Motherhood is bidding farewell to your original self and celebrating your reinvention. We, as mothers, reinvent ourselves to the new and vital task at hand. To the new call. To the new purpose. To the idea. And to the expectations others have of us and those we have about ourselves. This new purpose brings a whole new superpower to us mothers—the power of becoming that role model, which, ultimately, enables us to transform into better versions of ourselves. I am unaware of the existence of another superpower as meaningful as that of motherhood.

The sense of purpose inherited from motherhood is unique because it is not about a mother's actions but rather the impact those actions have on others. Along with motherhood comes an entirely different set of challenges, lessons, emotions, and the like. And when a Wall Street career is at the core of what you think defines you, everything becomes more challenging. Then you discover that you do not know much about life in general. Cheers to more learning and transformation!

Chapter 8

BOUNDARIES

...it is up to us to understand, accept, and communicate our boundaries. Once this is done, it is on others to respect them.

ONE DAY, I DROVE around my house in a corner lot and saw what looked like a wild animal trap between some of my shrubs on the side of my home. I thought it looked weird. But then I remembered the pest control company visited us a few days before, so I thought: "Let me call them to ensure this is their pest trap, not just an animal trap." The thought of catching an innocent animal in a trap makes me sick. I called the pest control company and asked if they placed that trap in my yard. They said: "No. The trap isn't ours." I got a little confused and worried. I thought to myself, *What if the kids were playing here during these days and tried to touch it? They could have gotten hurt. Why do I not know what this is, but it's on my property?* Desperate to solve this mysterious puzzle, I showed the trap picture to Noah. Noah immediately said, "This must be Robert's." Robert is our neighbor.

I said: "Really? Why wouldn't he tell or ask us before placing this here?"

Noah said: "No idea. He has done it before."

I felt invaded. How have I never noticed that before? Probably because I was never home, and when I was, I worked all the time. I never realized Robert habitually placed wild animal traps on our lawn. But I would expect a heads-up. Some sort of "Hey guys. I saw some interesting creatures roaming around, so I wondered if I could place a wild animal trap on your property?" Or: "Hey guys, would you be okay if I placed this trap on your property?" Something. A word. Say something. It is my property, after all. I have children who play freely in our front and backyard. So I got angry and defensive. I got scared. What if one of my children, out of innocent and genuine curiosity, touched this trap and got hurt? What then? Without drawing any precipitated conclusions, trying to manage my anxiety, and in an attempt to solve this mystery, I messaged Robert.

Ladyane: "Hi Robert, is this yours?" followed by a picture of the trap.

Robert: "Yes."

Ladyane: "Robert, could you please remove it from our property? If you want to place it on our lawn again, please let us know beforehand. Thanks!"

Robert: "K"

I solved my wild animal trap mystery, but someone violated my boundaries. I wished this wasn't happening. I love my neighbors, and I love my neighborhood. Without thinking much, I messaged Robert back. I needed him to know I would disapprove of putting a wild animal trap on my property. I did not feel the need to explain my reasons, but I thought one of them was obvious—I have small children who freely play in our front and backyard, and they could accidentally hurt themselves. Once I sent the message, there was no turning back. My hands shook while setting my much-needed (and maybe long overdue) boundary. I do not like setting boundaries. I have a problem doing it because it makes the other person feel something that, most of the time, is uncomfortable.

I do not like being the reason another person is in any sort of discomfort. I also don't like setting boundaries because it is a way to tell the other person, "Hey, you have done something that crossed my personal limit, and it makes me uncomfortable. You have made me very sad and/or very anxious. And that's because what you have done violates my set of beliefs and hurts me internally, on some level." So, when we set boundaries, we expose ourselves. We say a lot about ourselves to people who, sometimes, for some reason, do not even need to know us on that level or at all, for that matter.

I am still working on getting better at setting boundaries. With time and practice, I now understand that setting boundaries is essential for my emotional sanity. Without boundaries, others may get too comfortable at our emotional expense, which is unhealthy. Without explicitly setting boundaries, we are consumed by abusive dynamics, uncomfortable dialogues, and overwhelming emotions, all of which we are left alone to deal with. There is a silver lining, though - vulnerability is a source of strength. It is a source of potential. Setting boundaries makes us stronger.

Alright, friend, let me regale you with the saga of how I didn't exactly become a boundary expert overnight! Life is so marvelous that I have actually had plenty of opportunities to set boundaries, but I did not. From career to friendships and motherhood, life is about boundaries!

The Unpleasant Phone Call

I will share with you a few times when I should have set some boundaries in my career, but I did not. To simplify things, let's refer to the bank where I started my career right after college as Bank 1. The Bank where I joined William is Bank 2. I later joined what I call an European Bank.

One time, when I was already an Associate, I was preparing a presentation deck for the head of my department. My manager, a Vice President at the time, was working from home that day. She emailed me with directions about the presentation deck and let me run with it. She usually did not get on top of me to ensure the work was done. That day, unexpectedly, she did. She called me a few times and sounded edgy. I did not want to ask if everything was okay, I knew my boundaries. We did not have a close and personal relationship, not from my perspective. I figured if the presentation deck did not look how she wanted, she would call me and point it out so I could make the changes. No. That's not what happened. I sent her the last draft, and the next thing I knew, she was on the other side of the phone, raising her voice at me like I was her sister or a close relative: "What is this? How can I present this to them? My coworker could hear her yelling and looked at me in shock. I looked at him with the face of "I have no idea where this is coming from."

I tried to keep my professional composure and focus on her feedback, but it did not make sense because she sounded hysterical. I tried not to take it personally, but how can you not take it personally? She violated my professional and personal boundaries (never yell at someone and never lose your composure at work). I fixed the deck with her edgy direction, which, ultimately, was just a matter of adding one more dot to the existing timeline I had created. After I delivered the deck, I realized I was angry and sad. I let it sink in. I let it all sink in.

While trying to process and rationalize her behavior, I wondered if something was affecting her outside of work. However, I was on the front line and bore the brunt of her anger. Despite that, it didn't make her actions right. Below is my journal note from that day, where I attempted to rehearse what I was planning to say to her — but it never made it off paper. I never openly expressed how frustrated I felt with her lack of professionalism.

But I was hoping we could communicate about these things without me being yelled at. It is frustrating that sometimes I do not understand something or may not get the picture you are drawing, but I was hoping we

*could address this without making me uncomfortable with how you speak
to me.*

This journal excerpt stayed on the paper. I never had this conversation
with the manager who raised her voice at me. I never set my boundaries.
A few weeks later, she announced her first pregnancy so I concluded she
was going through a lot personally. Still, I did not set my boundaries. I
could have organised a quick fifteen-minute meeting with her to clarify
that I would like the tone to be consistent to avoid miscommunication.
I would then give this incident as an example and say I wish this would
not happen again. Short and sweet.

A few months later, I found out I was pregnant of Juliette. I decided to
announce my first pregnancy at work after my first trimester. So, I needed
to endure the fatigue, the nausea, and the doctor appointments secretly.
One day, I needed to leave a bit earlier because of a doctor's appointment.
A week or so later, I called in sick at work—which, most of the time, in
Wall Street, means I will work from home. So I logged in, and that same
manager messaged me, saying something like wanting to know if I was
pregnant because if I were, she needed to find a replacement for me while
I went on maternity leave.

Boundary violation alert! Boundaries are very personal. They vary
depending on your belief system, your culture, and who you are within
your soul. Boundaries differ based on our upbringing and experiences.
But it is up to us to understand, accept, and communicate our boundaries. Once this is done, it is on others to respect them.

None of the women I knew back on Wall Street had ever announced
their pregnancies before their first trimester was over. There are too
many variables and uncertainties during the first trimester, so, out of
precaution, I wanted to keep it in and share it only with our families.
As far as I knew, I did not need to tell my manager about my pregnancy
until after my first trimester. I wasn't breaking any rules. But I failed my
manager's expectations. I was in disbelief.

So, I did not tell her I was pregnant — I did not have to do that at that point in my pregnancy. I simply replied, "Can you imagine?"

Another valuable lesson my father taught me in our little time together was: "You cannot control how people behave with you. But you can control how you behave with them." I logged out that day feeling anxious because I thought I had lied to my manager. But I did not. I was upset because I thought I was doing something wrong. I thought I was hiding something that I shouldn't. But I should. It took me some processing time to understand that I was a private person; therefore, my manager's comment violated my privacy. I kept telling myself, *It's okay. Tell them at your own pace. You are not doing anything wrong.*

I cried a bit—hormones were all over. Noah hugged me all night and told me: "She is clueless." It was a big emotional wave. I surrendered to the big feelings and let them all out. The next day, I was in the office and ready to be productive, as if nothing had happened. I could not control what my manager wrote or said to me, but I could control how I behaved towards her. I announced my first pregnancy two months later with a massive smile, and I felt proud of myself for keeping my private life to myself and not yelling at anyone in the process.

I am uncertain how I could have handled my manager's lack of empathy and awareness at that time, it is tricky to address. Today, I feel that I did my best with what I had. Lately, however, I have been thinking about boundaries and how they could impact my children. So I feel that if this pregnancy episode happened to one of my daughters and they felt strong about their private lives like I did back then, I would give them a big hug and listen to them. I would then tell them to wait until they are ready to announce the biggest joy of their lives to the outer world.

Or, maybe my daughters will not have the same type of boundary I have. Who knows? But this was a matter of privacy and health, which has nothing to do with how soon my manager could find a replacement for me. Nothing more to it.

Six months later, I gave birth to the most beautiful and perfect baby girl. It was on 5th Avenue, facing Central Park, New York City. It was just me, Noah, my doctor, and baby Juliette. It was beautiful. It was magical. Juliette came in slowly but surely. She allowed me to touch her while I was still pushing. And as soon as we locked each other's eyes, there I was, surrendered with my heart and soul. That's when I understood the meaning of being the heart and soul of another human being.

Motherhood & Another Unpleasant Chat - Part II

When I gave birth to Juliette I was still an associate at Bank 1. Halfway through my maternity leave, William called me to check on me and ask if I would be interested in returning to Bank 2 and joining a new team with more structure. I can't lie. The recognition of the quality of my work was a motivation for me. Who wouldn't want to know that their work is appreciated and wanted? William followed by saying that the team was more structured. I asked a few details about what he would need me to do. He said he needed me to lead the transition of the Latin American regulatory business from Brazil to the United States, so my Portuguese, Spanish, and cultural background would be extremely helpful. I said this sounded interesting (internally, I was thinking: Oh my god, this is a fantastic opportunity). I told him I needed time to think.

So I thought about it, did some math, talked to my mentor, and brainstormed with Noah. A few days later, William and I spoke, and I said something like this: "I want X amount of money (thinking we were going to settle in the middle), work from home three days a week, and make me Vice President at the end of the next year. Can you do that?" William said he needed to check the numbers, but everything else was a "go." A few hours later, we agreed on a number. I decided to return from maternity leave to Bank 1 so that they could perhaps give me a counteroffer and, in a failed attempt, not burn any professional bridges. I made a mistake. And I will tell you how bad it was.

I had an easy but chaotic maternity leave. I barely slept, was always alert, and checked every breath Juliette took. I was exhausted but happy and fulfilled. Noah needed to travel a few times for work, but luckily, my mom, who had recently retired in Brazil, was staying with us to help us with everything.

I took my time to process motherhood. I took the time to get to know Juliette. I created a feeding, sleeping, and playtime routine. There was a schedule. My goal was to leave everything set so I could peacefully return to work. I wanted the Vice President title and wanted to buy our home. Baby Juliette, Noah, and I got a routine going and we taught each other some valuable lessons. Noah taught me how to change her diaper. Juliette taught me how to be less perfectionist. Noah gave her baths. I would feed her dinner. Noah would read to her at bedtime. We would then cuddle, and I sang to her until she fell asleep in my arms. After I accepted the fact that I was allowed to rest and be a real mom, Noah, Juliette, and I created a fantastic routine and bond. We were a team. I will forever want to remember the transformation from boyfriend and girlfriend into father and mother—it was challenging. It took us some time to get the hang of it. There were days when we felt that nothing we were doing was right. There were days when I questioned my marriage. Nothing prepares a couple for the first months of a firstborn. I learned that you must be able to see yourself and your partner beyond that transitional and special phase; it is rewarding. It is fulfilling. It is challenging, but it is magical. Today, when I think of those days, I know I would do everything over again exactly as I did it. There was a reason for the questions, for the challenges, and for the lessons learned.

We started looking at daycares before Juliette was born. As the time to return to work was approaching, I started panicking. At each daycare I visited, I could only think about how terrifying it was and worry that my baby girl might be neglected. It isn't true, though. This was just what my mind was telling me. None of the daycares checked the boxes for me. They were wonderful places. I just wasn't brave enough to leave baby Juliette in daycare to return to work. I couldn't justify it. I am in awe and deeply admire and respect mothers who manage to execute this difficult task; it isn't easy to leave your baby in a daycare, but they do it anyway. They already know it isn't easy, but it's magical. I created an unpleasant truth in my head about daycares so that I could justify to myself not sending Juliette to one—that's the truth. Remember when I said some truths are unpleasant, but recognizing and accepting them is liberating? I will tell you how.

In desperation mode, from one mother to another, I made an offer to my mom: She would take care of Juliette for us while we worked, and I would pay her for it. As a new retiree with no plans for the near future, I figured: *Why not be a present grandmother while I try to have a career on Wall Street with peace of mind?* If it worked out for all of us and she wanted to stay longer, I would then apply for her visa extension and, ultimately, apply for her green card so she could have the option to rebuild her life in the US. She happily said, "Yes!" One of the best decisions I have made in my life—having my mother, who is an integral part of my supporting village, right beside me changed my life. And better, being able to provide her with options out of opportunities and not necessities made me feel I could close that circle in her life. It made me feel I could give her something I thought she deserved for all her sacrifices to raise me with dignity and integrity.

Let's pause here, friend. We often associate fear with negativity. But when we do not dismiss or try to avoid fear and instead become aware of it, accept it, and respect it, we can control it. And when we can control fear, we can do wonderful things. In the past, Ladyane would deal with fear by ignoring its existence; I did not even allow myself to recognize and manage it. This time around, I saw myself doing something different with that fear. I turned the fear of leaving Juliette in daycare into bravery by offering my mother the option of trying to rebuild a new life in the US. On her terms, out of her options and not necessities. Elizabeth Gilbert offers a motivating perspective about fear in her book, *The Big Magic*. She says she has prepared a welcoming speech to fear whenever she is about to begin a new project or adventurous endeavor. How amazing is this? In the context of a road trip, Gilbert says that fear is forbidden from taking the driver's seat and should not make any decisions along the way. However, Gilbert recognizes and respects fear's presence. Retroactively, I did precisely that by accepting my unpleasant truth of fearing sending baby Juliette to daycare but going around and saying: "I will think of something that will not compromise my emotional safety yet allow me to return to work peacefully."

When I returned to Bank 1 from maternity leave, I informed them I had an offer to join Bank 2 and would be willing to stay if they could match the offer. It was a mistake—realistically, Bank 1 could not match the title and the associated salary. But I naively thought I could stay if they gave me a work-from-home arrangement. The head of the department heard about my offer and asked to meet with me. I thought she would say something like: "Congratulations on your baby girl! Unfortunately, we cannot match the offer. We are sad, but we wish you the best of luck." She did the exact opposite. The exchange went something like this:

Margaret: "So, I hear you have an offer to join Bank 2."

Ladyane: "Yes – I do. The work-from-home arrangement appeals to me because I could use that time with my baby. Not having to commute a few days a week would be great with a newborn at home."

Margaret: "Well, I do not see how we can do that, nor do I think this would be a good move for your career progression here. This arrangement could impact your ability to get promoted to Vice President."

Ladyane: "Really? How come?" (I was confused, so I figured I should ask).

Margaret: "We do not have this culture here in the team."

Ladyane: "I see. I thought we could work something out for at least the first six months. After the first six months, I could gradually return to the office for all five days." (I was confused why we were even associating my ability to get promoted with my work arrangement and not with the quality of my work).

Margaret: "Yeah, it won't happen here."

Her tone, expressing disappointment about me leaving the team, made me feel as if I were betraying her.

All I could say was: "Okay, Margaret. I understand."

I lied. I did not understand it. How could my desire to work from home impact my chances of promotion more than the quality of my work? It didn't make sense to me.

I stepped out of her office and went to my desk. I sat down and looked at the computer screen.

Breathe in, Ladyane. Breathe out.

What's coming up for me? *Remember your trajectory, Ladyane. Think about the destination.*

Staring at those two computer screens—one screen with two spreadsheets opened beside each other, another with a presentation deck and a meeting reminder popping up saying I was two minutes late for the call—all sharing two big monitors—I realized I felt relieved. I stood up and went to wash my face. I joined the call ten minutes later.

I resigned from Bank 1 that day. I figured there was no time to waste. I knew I did not want to work for a woman who did not support another woman in the workplace. I knew my request to work from home was neither unrealistic nor impossible. I also understood that it shouldn't affect my chances of promotion, as promotions should be based on work quality and professional performance. We all experienced this firsthand when COVID-19 hit hard in 2020, forcing everyone to work from home. I've never worked as much as I did in 2020, and it was all done remotely. It just so happens that a particular professional leading that particular team within that big global bank was a toxic professional. We always come across a toxic professional at some point, no matter what industry we work in. In fact, we always come across toxic people, no matter how hard we try to avoid them. The purpose is to learn from them what not to do and move on with our lives with grace and peace. I also knew she didn't represent the entire bank's culture, as my professional trajectory there was outstanding, thanks to the many remarkable leaders I had the privilege to work with.

Two weeks later, I packed my belongings, bid farewell, and took some time off to happily transition from Bank 1 to Bank 2. Bank 2 afforded me more financial freedom, stability, and the title of Vice President.

Mama Brasicana—Brazilian and American Mama & The Labor of Love

So that they fully understand that parenting labor is not fast-paced, emotionally distant, juggling, and struggling with everyday labor but simply a labor of love.

Shortly after Juliette turned one, Noah and I purchased our first home in the suburbs of New Jersey. I had overcome my fear of sending her to daycare, and we were pregnant with our baby boy. Sometimes, when we face fear, we just need to sit still and be. All we can do is allow ourselves to feel it and let it manifest itself. Fear is not a bad thing, it prevents us from getting hurt. So, I sat on that fear for a while, while I tackled other battles.

Juliette started attending daycare a few months after we moved to the suburbs. The daycare was a short two-minute walk from our house. I could see the playground she played with her friends and teachers from her bedroom window. Peeking at her playing in the playground in the middle of the day made me feel like I had won the lottery—being able to do that made me feel less afraid. One day, Juliette's teacher approached me at pick-up time and said: "You must stop speaking your first language with J at home. She cannot communicate with us and doesn't understand what we are telling her."

Ladyane, are you there? Breathe.

Stop. *What did this woman just say?* "Sorry, what did you say?"

Teacher: "She cannot understand what we are telling her. You got to stop speaking your language with her."

Ladyane: "Okay." I nodded.

I picked Juliette up and went back home. During the short walk back home, holding my almost two-year-old daughter's hand, heart racing, and hands shaking, I thought: *Why? What's wrong with me speaking Portuguese to Juliette? Why did I just hear a stranger tell me I should not speak my first language with my daughter in my home? This teacher has just crossed so many boundaries.* The audacity to say to me, an immigrant mother, to stop speaking my first language with my daughter was beyond what I could ever imagine.

A gigantic emotional wave. I was anxious. I was asking myself *Am I harming my daughter by only talking to her in my first language?* I did not know any better back then. Noah and I spoke and agreed that this teacher had indeed crossed a boundary. We asked to meet with the teacher and the daycare director to set some boundaries and expectations. We wanted the experience in daycare to work for all of us. In the meeting, I tried not to do most of the talking; I was still angry at the teacher, and nothing good would come out of my mouth if I were to talk. It got way too personal. So Noah took on the role of spokesperson: "We didn't want to have to clarify what languages we speak in our own home with our daughter, but I guess we will have to do it to set our expectations about you guys. We do not only speak Portuguese with Juliette at home. I am not Brazilian, so I speak English with Juliette. But this is all irrelevant because our expectation of you as a teacher is that you will be patient and provide the best care regardless of the child's ability to communicate. This is Juliette's first experience in a social setting like this, so we know she needs time to trust and adjust to the new place and new people. We expect that you will make her feel comfortable. Do you guys have anything to add?"

When Noah started talking, I could tell he was furious. But he kept going and was much more in control than I was. So he went on with: "I hope we clarify that the language barrier piece and what language we communicate with our daughter is irrelevant to her adjustment process here. We trust that you will make Juliette feel comfortable here."

The director immediately apologized for the "misunderstanding." She followed by saying that they loved having Juliette and that they would ensure the transition would be subtle and happy. The teacher did not speak. We left the meeting with the common understanding that the teacher should have never asked me to stop speaking my first language with my daughter.

Seeing Noah speak nonstop at that meeting, almost as if he were an attorney advocating for his client, made me realize, right there and then, that we were going through a test. Watching my husband fiercely yet respectfully stand up for our multicultural family made me realize the unique challenges of raising children with a strong cultural legacy in America. I knew then that I had to be ready to face similar situations in the future. I also realized that I was going to embrace the labels others may place on us simply because by doing that, I then have an opening to share our story — how an Israeli guy and a Brazilian girl fell in love and built a family rooted in curiosity, laughter and a deep respect for diversity.

Our blend of cultures is a gift to our children. One I am proud to pass on.

Later that day, after we put Juliette to sleep, Noah and I hugged and laughed at the thought of going through that same episode again; our baby boy was on the way, and we knew the journey would be long. But we were ready for it — We knew we shared the same love, values, and meaning which would ultimately ignite us to embrace the challenges and keep going. That hug felt safe. That hug screamed emotional stability.

A lot of people associate motherhood with the end of a cycle. End of freedom. End of a carefree life. I argue that motherhood means the actual opposite. Every time a woman gives birth, she is reborn. This new version of herself has the opportunity to become whoever she's always wanted to be because she is transformed. Quietly yet powerfully, she finds new meaning. She rises and becomes greater in everything she undertakes. After all, she has another new, most important task. That is, the one to raise a child with intention. To put it simply, no child is the same as the other. No woman is the same as the one she was before giving birth.

Friend, there is a word in Hebrew called *kavanah*. I learned about kavanah in the early days of my conversion process. Kavanah refers to the intention, focus, and devotion one brings to one's daily life. It highlights the importance of being present at the moment, connecting to one's intention, and transforming ordinary daily activities into an opportunity to connect to yourself or someone else on a deeper level. In short, kavanah encourages me to think about my intentions when connecting with others. I ultimately ask myself: "What is my intention here?" There is power in asking yourself this question because, more often than not, we do not fully understand why we do things the way we do them, and why we do them in the first place, and this happens because we are simply on autopilot.

I became a mother of two in January of 2018. It was a cold January Monday. Baby Gabriel was a big boy, full of energy and light. Just like with Juliette, his birth was magical. And somewhat more predictable. But, you see, friend, no matter how much we prepare or plan, things are just meant to happen for reasons you may understand only later in life. In the birth room, baby Gabriel wanted to take his time while I was pushing. In exhaustion, due to the excessive pushing, I turned to the doctor and, gasping for air, and said: "Doctor, take me to the surgery room; we need to go with a C-section. I can't push anymore." I did not have any more strength to keep pushing. The doctor looked me in the eyes and said: "Ladyane, you are a perfectly healthy woman, and your baby is perfect. I can see his head already. Just two more big pushes. You can do this."

Meanwhile, Noah whispered, "Buba, you can do this. You are amazing. He is almost here. I can see him. You can do it. You can do it." I caught my breath and started praying as if I already had Gabriel in my arms—I could feel him in my arms. I caught my breath and gave two other big pushes, and the next thing I knew, Gabriel was in my arms, inspecting every inch of my face while the doctor and the nurse were cheering and saying: "You did it, guys! He is amazing, Mama. And you are powerful." The room was full of smiles, joy, and cheering.

I can still remember Gabriel's smell. The adrenaline of holding my big baby boy as if that was a re-encounter and not a "Pleased to meet you." It was as if we told each other, "It was about time, right?" While Noah was crying, he smiled and said: "You are amazing, Buba. Look at our baby boy. He is perfect." Later that day, while eating dinner and breastfeeding baby Gabriel, I told Noah that those words he whispered in my ear had so much intention that empowered me to give those two big pushes. Present at that moment, holding Gabriel, connecting with him as if we were telling each other: "Hey, so amazing to see you again." I realized I had just become a new woman and that it was time for me to start manifesting that latest version of myself—a more resilient, aware, present, and less controlling Ladyane.

Gabriel is truly a burst of joy. He is our wave in the sense that he gives us calm; when he looks at us, all we can see is the constant reminder that there is always a calm wave that we ride after a huge one. Gabriel is genuine and charismatic. Gabriel has tons of empathy, he is the type of kid who will ask if you are okay if he sees you struggle with something. Gabriel genuinely cares. He provides us comfort when we need it. And some more, even when we don't. He is a bear, he loves hugs and affection. He gives us the giggles in the most unexpected moments. He loves chatting about movies, math, the solar system, and playing the piano. He loves playing UNO and chess. In his bedroom wall is a wall art painted blue that says: "Ride The Wave." One day, Gabriel and I were sitting at the dining table finishing our breakfast, and I had a short chat with him that made me realize the intention is present and manifesting itself—the chat went something like this:

Ladyane: "You guys are so lucky. You can spend the summer days with your friends, playing together and having fun at summer camp. I did not have summer camp when I was growing up.

Gabriel: "Mommy, did summer camps not exist when you were a kid?"

Ladyane: "They did, but Grandmother could not afford to put me in summer camp. So, I spent the summer days at my godmother's house while my mom worked. My godmother used to watch after me."

Pause. Silence. Gabriel looks like he is processing the input I just gave him. Nothing happens for half a minute. And, suddenly, Gabriel looks at me:

Gabriel: "Humm, I think you are the lucky one."

Ladyane: "How come, Gabriel?"

Gabriel: "Humm, well, Mommy, you got to spend your summer days with someone who loved you deeply. That's good stuff."

Pause. I needed to process the emotional load of information my six-year-old had just candidly shared with me. The thorough process that

Gabriel applied to come up with that conclusion required a response at the same level. So, I took my time to get everything right. I did some deep thinking to provide him with an answer that would meet him at the same emotional level. I did some retroactive thinking to fully understand the impact of what I was about to say. Do you know what that is, friend? Intention. Emotional intention. The chat proceeded with something like this:

Ladyane: "Gabriel, you are very right. I was very lucky. In that case, I then believe you have double the luck. You get to spend half of your day playing with your best friends, and then you spend the other half with me. How amazing is this?"

Gabriel: "You bet it is. I am super lucky." Followed by a big smile, giggle, and ready for his second breakfast round, he says, "Can I please have Cheerios with milk?"

I looked at Noah, who witnessed the entire chat from the kitchen, and we both made eye contact as if we were telling one another, *Goodness, we may not have it all figured out, but we must be up to something good over here.*

As per my definition, Mama Brasicana is a Brazilian mom who has physically left Brazil for different reasons but persists in carrying on her emotional legacy for the benefit of her children. Each Brazilian mother who comes to the US and attempts to raise a child has her journey, triumphs, and challenges. Lessons learned and doubts. Fears and joys. For that, she has left all her old self in her home country while consistently trying to reinvent herself each day in a new country, with new people, and in a new culture; this, in itself, is the definition of transformation.

A Mama Brasicana believes that for her children to know who she is as a mother, they must understand where she comes from and appreciate her journey. This mama constantly exposes her children to the culture in which she has been raised. She lectures her children on the lessons her parents taught her. To this day, almost every time I take my kids to swimming lessons, I tell them, "Grandpa thought this was a life skill! Wouldn't you agree? Go for it!"—an example of my attempt to share with them what I learned from my father in our short time together. They look at me as if I am crazy and say: "Yes, Mommy. You say this every time you bring us to swimming practice."

But why does this all matter? Why is being a Mama Brasicana so relevant? Why is it so important to carry on this legacy that, technically, does not belong to my children? After all, they are Americans. Yes, they are—born and raised. However, I must pass on the emotional legacy to them so they can fully appreciate the choices, values, and emotional intentions I bring to raising them. I do not foresee a life in Brazil for my children, although the option is available when and if they choose. But I hope that when I am mothering, they will understand my emotions because of where I come from. And they can only do that if I share my journey, the lessons I learned from a Ladyane they have never met and have no idea existed before they were born. I can't simply wipe my old Brazilian self out of my identity. Instead, I share it with them so we can connect emotionally. You see, when I realized I could raise my children this way, it was like a light bulb in my head. Everything started making sense. And everything became a bit more challenging.

Every day, I make choices that mix and match all cultures. Not in an attempt to alienate them from the American culture. But to help them understand who Daddy and Mommy were before they were born, and to help them understand the values and lessons we try to teach them. My chat with Gabriel about summer days makes one of the lessons obvious—cherish the time you spend with those you love. Make the most of it. It doesn't matter where you are and how much you have in your bank account (they don't fully understand the concept of budgeting yet, although it is something we practice with them). But they do know that part of who we are has to do with having just enough for as long as we have emotional and physical integrity and an overload of love.

Friend, there is power in each one of our journeys, and I urge us to share our journeys with our children so that they can have a shot at fully comprehending who we are and why we teach specific lessons. Being emotionally intentional with our children has very little to do with what we do for a living and how we pay our bills. It has nothing to do with the title we have at work, the industry we work in, or the number of zeros in the bank account. It has to do with connecting intentionally with our children so that there is an exchange of love. So that they fully understand that parenting labor is not fast-paced, emotionally distant, juggling, and struggling with everyday labor, but simply a labor of love.

Chapter 9

THE DAY I BECAME A VICE PRESIDENT ON WALL STREET

Living the dream, Ladyane! Living the dream.

I WAS ON AUTOPILOT throughout my entire Wall Street career. I mainly focused on doing and rarely considered the actual being. I didn't sit still to think about whether that career was what I wanted to do. I didn't consider whether I, indeed, liked the environment. I liked the money, and I liked the stability it provided me.

Consequently, I did not take care of my emotional self well enough. How could I? I was constantly in fight-or-flight mode. I had financial goals and feared not being financially stable again. I did not consider the red flags that the working environment was showing me. So, I carried on the best I could. I simply manifested what I wanted—a stable financial life and the Vice President title. Given my upbringing, I wanted to create and set my safety zone, which I could not have accomplished in Brazil.

It was a Wednesday morning, and I could hear the lawnmowers all on at once. A few months after moving into the suburbs, I found the noise soothing. I logged in at around 7 a.m., and a bit after 8 a.m., I pinged William to have a candid conversation with him. It was almost as if he knew what I wanted to talk about. I started by telling him that I was halfway through my second pregnancy with baby Gabriel and commuting to the office was a struggle—the commute was long and much more challenging during the summer months. William anticipated the ask by saying: "You want to just work from home then?" I was relieved. I said: "Yes – it will be better for me and the team, too." He said that this was no problem—and he did not tell me working from home towards the end of my pregnancy would impact my ability to get promoted. I saw the full-time working-from-home arrangement as an opportunity for my work to shine—I started working at 6 or 7 a.m. and would log out at 5 p.m. to prepare Juliette for the evening routine.

During my entire Wall Street career and those 10 plus hours of intense daily work-from-home days, I developed a couple of habits that allowed me to advance professionally and build a good reputation with those I worked with. Friend, what I will share with you may create emotional burnout if used in abundance. So I warn you, engage carefully, and, once in a while, ask yourself, "What is my intention?" The habits I list below became part of who I was professionally—the only problem is that I did not know how to balance them out with the other roles I played in life, the mother role, for example. Ready?

Here are ten habits I found critical for achieving a successful career on Wall Street:

1. **I never said, "No, I cannot do it"** – On the contrary, I took ownership of almost everything that came my way. If a request was unrealistic, I challenged it with data or previous organizational experience. More on that below.

2. **I never said, "I do not know how to do this"** – Instead, I would say, "Let me look into it and get back to you." Or, "Yes—I can do it." I would then quickly teach myself a new skill.

3. **I connected with people** – I always had one-on-one meetings with my managers, my manager's manager, and my peers. You want to be in the loop about the general sentiment in the organization on a micro and macro level. Why? First, you want to understand the organizational strategy on a high level so that you know where you fit, and you can align your goals accordingly. Second, you want to carve out a specific persona to connect with each person you work with—people are different, so they need different versions of you. The latter is significant because you want to expand your professional network with various stakeholders. Remember: The supporting village begins early in your career, and you want to have those key people (sponsors, mentors, connectors) next to you. Besides, in big organizations, you always need something from someone. Connection is key to advancing your career and expanding possibilities.

4. **I never disagreed unprofessionally** – Remember when I said one of my managers used to say I was a "sweet talker"? Yes, I disagreed by agreeing. How do you do that? I validated people's opinions and sentiments. I listened to them and tried to make them shine. People like to be heard, understood, and validated –in *any* relationship you develop, not just professionally. Still, I carried on with my agenda, always substantiated with data (so I did a lot of homework), or by previous organizational experiences.

5. **I tried not to take things personally** – After the incident

with the manager who yelled at me over the phone, I figured, "It's not personal." Later in my career, I would get calls from traders yelling at me, asking me why they couldn't trade a specific share. Telling me I was not helping the business. I would, in return, sympathize with their frustration, explain again why they couldn't trade, and finish the call on a professional note. I guess one could argue that my Wall Street career taught me a bit of emotional control, and I am thankful for that. Now, friend, repeat: "It's not personal."

6. **I always raised my hand** – I would always raise my hand to take on the ownership of a new project or initiative. I liked the pressure and the exposure—I saw it as an opportunity for the senior team to see me. It also helped me expand my network within the banks and the industry.

7. **Directly related to no. 6, I managed my time efficiently** – I kept a working spreadsheet of everything I was responsible for and my oversight work. I tagged an average weekly time on each task and its deadline. I always set my deadline a few days before the agreed-upon deadline. This way, I not only knew how much time and effort I spent on each task and project but could complete deliverables ahead of the deadline agreed upon with my manager or other stakeholders. Managers used to defer to me to understand if we could take on new initiatives. You can accomplish many wins when you know how to manage your time.

8. **I knew my stuff** – With the spreadsheet of what I was working on, I was always able to pitch my work and how it impacted the organization any time the opportunity arose. You never know who you will bump into when grabbing a coffee or water or

inside the elevator. Knowing what you are up to and speaking with authority about your work can take you far.

9. **I never feared organizational changes and pivoting strategies** – Instead, I embraced them and showed enthusiasm. Let's be honest, someone had already made the decision for organizational change. Unless this decision threatens the existence of your role, then the best thing to do is to embrace the change, navigate the change, and adapt. Or, even better, lead the change. Be an agent of change, and lead the new version of the organization by example.

10. **Lastly, I was always professional** – A fast-paced and stressful work environment can bring out the worst in people — Do not let that drag you down. Take control. Keep it up even if someone does or says something that may cross your boundary. Carry on professionally. The way they behave speaks more about them than about yourself. I am not saying you should ignore your emotions. Still, it is important to differentiate what a not-so-professional incident means professionally and personally—two different layers. Hence, they need to be handled differently. I am also not saying you should be a robot—connect, but do not cross a line unless the other party gives you room. Being professional is something we practice, and just like a muscle, it becomes a habit and genuine. I will provide an example: In emails, when I needed something from someone, I would always write: *"Could I kindly ask you to..."* I know it's simple, but it makes a huge difference. I never had to ask something from others more than once. I know this is a simple example, but it shows the level of professionalism the other person is about to encounter if he or she were to call you to ask more about your inquiry. Keep it professional and straightfor-

ward. Feel them out before you assume anything.

A few days before the promotion/communication day, a day dedicated to communicating work performance, salary, and promotion, William and I met at a diner by my house. He talked to me about the organizational plans, where he wanted my focus, what other team members would focus on, and strategies. A few days later, and about two weeks before I gave birth to baby Gabriel, we had the promotion call, and it went something like this: "Based on all your dedication and everything you helped us accomplish, we are happy to promote you to Vice President. Well deserved, Ladyane."

And just like that, I started laughing loudly on the phone and failed to hear the salary and bonus numbers associated with the promotion William was just saying. As I asked William to repeat the numbers, he gleefully repeated them, and we both found ourselves in complete joy. Laughing, I said, "Ahhh, this feels good, William!" And William said, "Living the dream, Ladyane! Living the dream." The moment was extraordinary because the professional promoting me was someone who had witnessed my career ascension, knew precisely the challenges I had overcome on both personal and professional levels, and contributed to my career advancement. Not many people can share that moment with someone who was so essential and part of their professional career village.

We hung up, and I ran out of my home office straight to my kitchen and hugged my mom, saying: "I did it! I did it, Mom!" My mom was confused—she had no idea what had just happened. Laughing, she said, "What did you do?" and I said, "I got promoted to Vice President!" I showed her my phone screen displaying the promotion letter, which included the title and the numbers: "Look at these numbers!" And laughing, she said, "This is amazing! Congratulations, my dear."

That night, Noah and I talked about my trajectory and what things would look like moving forward—more work, responsibility, and autonomy. As the night went on Noah and I thought: What's next? I wanted to sit tight for a bit; I needed time to navigate the waters. Get a feel for what it would be like to be a Vice President officially. We both agreed that my motivations were changing as my journey was changing. During that chat, we discussed how we should not ignore the main drivers motivating us to work. We realized money, recognition, and passion/joy are the main drivers. I checked off the first two at that point in my career. I did not check the third one. As I got myself ready to sleep, in an attempt to know if I had checked the "passion" box, the thought lingered incessantly in my mind: *Do I feel fulfilled when I wake up every morning to go to work? Do I do what I do because I am passionate about it? Because I feel joy? Do I feel a purpose other than making money and getting recognition for my work?* Hang tight, friend. There is more. While I tried answering these questions as if the answers were day or night, I ended up realizing that this is not how things work in real life. Life is not linear.

The next couple of weeks, I debated whether I had hit the jackpot and whether I was working on something I was passionate about. At that point, I checked the box on money and recognition; I was doing well financially and was finally a Vice President at a top global investment bank. Yet, I was unhappy. You see, friend, the tricky part of you having such a promising career in a work environment where people feed your ego is that you sometimes trick yourself into thinking you are passionate about what you do. I think I did that until I started paying more attention to being in that environment and what that was doing to me at that point in my life as I embarked on a journey of being a mother of two.

I pondered for a while during the following days. I knew the promotion was a testament to my professional dedication. It symbolized the challenges I overcame—a young girl from Brazil with almost nothing, graduating from college with honors, and becoming Vice President at a top global investment bank a few years later. It felt good knowing that this was possible because I earned it. I worked hard, and I did it.

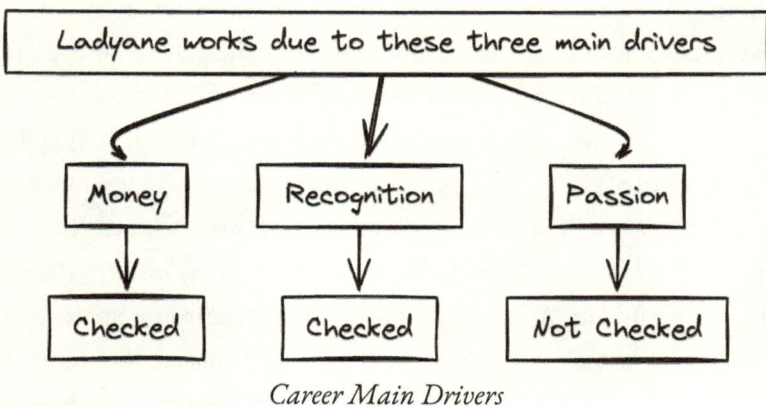

Career Main Drivers

Gabriel was born about two weeks after my promotion to Vice President. It was a cold winter January morning, and there I was, surrendered to the joy of having my baby boy in my arms and watching my daughter and husband delightfully smile at us both. At that moment, with that picture in my head, I decided I would create a storage compartment in my mind to save that career motivation thought for later. Contemplating the answer to that fundamental question required too much brain power for me to be able to answer if I was, indeed, passionate about what I had been doing for eight years. I was still looking at this question the wrong way.

Friend, picture this: There I was. I had just given birth to my baby boy. I was so profoundly joyful as I saw my family growing with two beautiful and healthy children that I simply did not have enough emotional space to keep contemplating the question: *Does this work bring me joy?* And just like when you have multiple tabs open on your laptop, and you cannot focus on them all at once, I decided to "minimize" all those career-related tabs for that time being. I decided to reassess the question when I got a better handle on being a mother of two. When I knew I could allow more mental space to topics other than my beautiful and growing family. I respected my boundaries—I set my pace. I craved the loving moments with my family. So, I left the question alone and focused on the task at hand—being able to be a good and intentional mother of two. After all, I was the heart and soul of my little people. I am thankful I did that, because it allowed me to recap my journey up to that point:

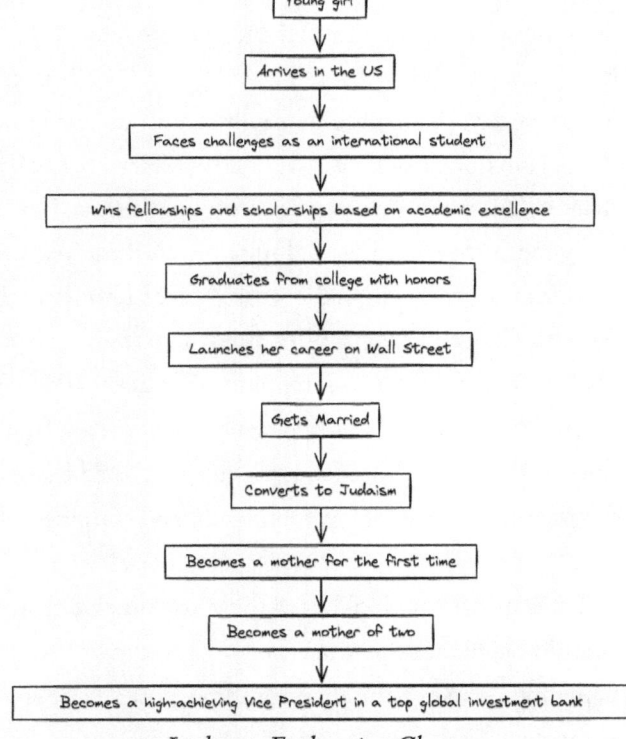

Ladyane Embracing Change

I Do Not Do Well With Farewell

My Wall Street career was a pivotal stepping stone that paved the way for the comfortable and fulfilling life I lead today.

Friend, as I endlessly pondered the question, "Does this feed my soul?" I realized I was afraid of the answer. And I realized I was looking at the answer the wrong way. Firstly, I feared answering "No." I feared that a "No" answer would cause a change I would regret. I feared a "No" answer would negatively impact me and my family. Back then, in my mind, I thought: "How could I possibly say "No"? After all the dedication and hard work I applied incessantly in my career? How could I ever say "No, I am not passionate about my work. It does not bring me joy?" Initially, in this inquisitive process, I thought that a "No" answer would simply mean that I had wasted my time all those years tricking myself into thinking I truly enjoyed my career, that I honestly thought my career was fulfilling and joyous. What I ended up realizing after much reflection is that, yes, my career was fulfilling. My career had fed my soul for as long as it served its purpose. My career brought me joy, fulfillment, and happiness for as long as I needed it to. I realized I had changed, and with that change, the sources of joy, fulfillment, and happiness changed as well.

You see, I was incorrectly looking at the question and answer. The question should be: "Does this work feed my soul now?" And "Is my work bringing me a sense of fulfillment and purpose?" The answers to these questions will change as life experiences transform us. We aren't meant to be the same every step of the way in life. We evolve.

I transformed. My needs and aspirations changed.
So, it was time to change.

I was determined to answer "Yes" to that question for a long time. For a long time, I thought I could not allow myself to understand and accept that the "Yes" was temporary and that it could change simply because I changed. My career did feed my soul. It did bring me joy. It did serve a purpose—to get myself and my growing family the financial stability

I did not have as a child. It gave me the fulfillment and stability I had craved all my young adult life. But I evolved.

My career and excessive dedication were mainly driven by the necessity to prevent history from repeating itself. To break a cycle. I never considered whether my career genuinely fulfilled me. To understand how to look at this question and be able to answer it, I studied the available literature about career development and personal fulfillment. This was when I bumped into the work of Bill Burnett and Dave Evans – they both wrote *Designing Your Life: How to Build a Well-lived, Joyful Life*. The book offers a framework and a process for building a joyful life. I was good at creating and following processes. I did that on Wall Street, so I figured, why not create my own process for tackling this life-changing decision I am about to make?

Two months had passed since I returned from maternity leave, and I just had the unpleasant meeting with my coworker who had a strong opinion about my reviewer role. My body and my mind were telling me that a change was about to happen.

Steady.

Strong.

Vigilant.

My mantra always came in handy when I had nowhere to run to. It allowed me to be in the moment. I wanted to listen to what was coming up for me in every interaction I had—with coworkers, mentors, friends, and family. All I needed to do was take that awareness and ask myself, "What's next, then?"

Crafting the way forward is a process. Following through that process requires self-awareness, discipline, and intention. The purpose will then reveal itself once we ask ourselves consistently: "What is my true intention and purpose here?" Think of it as if you commit to yourself—the same discipline we apply to other endeavors, like working out. Gradually, I came to grasp a profound truth about my purpose: my Wall Street career was a pivotal stepping stone that paved the way for the comfortable and fulfilling life I lead today.

I drafted a plan. My plan started with questions: Where do I see myself? What could the trade-off be if I were to take a sabbatical? What do I not want? What do I want? What kind of life do I want for my family after the sabbatical and onward? How can I start (re)designing my trajectory? In answering these questions, I concluded two things:

1. We can thrive at what we do regardless of being passionate about it. It is all about the trade-off. What do I gain and lose by doing this? I was not passionate about my daily Wall Street work, yet I was a high achiever. I enjoyed my work and career trajectory because I had a clear purpose. I associated meaning and purpose with my career, and along with the money and recognition components, I made the best out of it for as long as I needed it to. However, my trajectory changed when my body and mind started painting a different picture of what that career was bringing up to me.

2. Redesigning our life journeys to live our best lives is possible because of our life experiences, the challenges we overcome, our failures, and the lessons we constantly learn. Hence, I am confident that I would do it all over again— I would do it all over again simply because I accepted that my motto at a certain point in life was "Make money first, worry about true happiness later." The motto can change because we change, and accepting this process is beautiful, empowering, and liberating.

My problem is that once I started questioning myself about what would be next for me, I was afraid of leaving the certainty of a well-established and high-achieving Wall Street career. I was fearful of bidding farewell to a promising career. It was challenging to say goodbye to years of hard work and dedication; I had achieved so much and had learned a great deal. How could I simply say goodbye to Wall Street? How could I? I realized I did not want to bid farewell. I eventually decided that this would not be a "goodbye" but a "to be continued." Yet, thinking of taking a sabbatical and planning for it was scary. Because I was about to pause my motto, I was listening to my body and new purpose, which was terrifying and unusual. I was not ready to bid farewell to the high-achieving and intense Wall Street Ladyane. Yet, every time I would take a day off (whatever that meant those days) and get to spend time with my children, I would realize I missed the moments I wish I could have more of with them. I needed more balance between Wall Street Ladyane and Mother Ladyane; I needed to allow more space for Mother Ladyane to play her role more intentionally and less chaotically.

In the Spring of 2018, Gabriel was almost six months old, and Juliette was two years old. I had returned to work from maternity leave to find myself placed in a new function utterly different from what I used to do before going on maternity leave. To make things more challenging, part of my role in this new function was to arrive in the office at 7 a.m. I had to leave the house in the morning when my children were still asleep. By the time I would get back home after an exhausting day of work, the only time I had left with them was to take care of them and put them in bed. I missed the most precious moments of my baby boy waking up in the morning and my almost three-year-old girl. I was emotionally and physically exhausted. I was riding an enormous emotional wave and had no idea how to catch my breath. On a Summer evening in 2018, I sat down with Noah and showed him my exit/sabbatical plan strategy.

My idea was simple: I would do it in phases and create prototypes of what the new life could look like. In the paper, I had drafted a few questions, and one of them was: How could I take a sabbatical sometime in 2021 to be more present with my children? Noah was fully supportive—we planned. We budgeted. And we manifested the plan endless evenings, brainstorming some what-ifs. Noah repeated to me endless times: "This break will be a win-win for you and the family." We were both convinced that we were all going to benefit from it. Part of my exit strategy was to have a prototype of the future—in reality, this is how the prototype would look: I was going to find a role closer to our home so that I could cut on commuting time to be able to spend more quality time with the children and spend more time on myself. Cutting on commuting time was a big win for me, considering I used to spend more than two hours both ways to get to the office. I planned and executed. This gave me better control over my career. I created a spreadsheet with a list of banks and financial services institutions in our region; I started tapping my network to spread the news that I was open for new roles, and I started getting on calls with headhunters. The great gift of networking is that people start giving you different directions – all possibilities you can explore as your way forward. Below is a quick snapshot of what my plan consisted of:

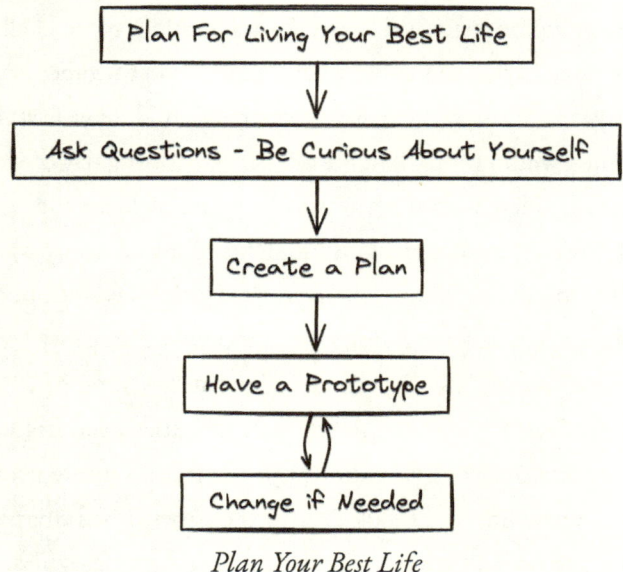

Plan Your Best Life

Curiosity enables us to see the path forward.

Plan Your Best Life

1 – Ask questions

Curiosity enables us to see the path forward. Here are a few examples of relevant questions:

- What is it about your life that you dislike today? Followed by: Can you act on it? In my case, I disliked that I missed doctor appointments (Noah had more flexibility); I definitely didn't like leaving the house so early to go to work and that impacted my ability to say "good morning" to my children.

- Is there something missing? If so, can you point your finger at it? Can you tell what your body tells you due to this deficit you are feeling? In my case, I missed having more quality time with my family.

- What do you wish you had more of? In my case, I wished I had more time for myself and my family. I also wished I had more flexibility to work from home due to the endless children-related events and other activities. I wished I could spend more time intentionally with my husband and children.

- What is my intention? In my case, I wanted to be more emotionally available to my family and wanted to, eventually, take a break to reset emotionally.

2 – Ask the follow-up questions

- What can I do about it?

- Can I act on it or pieces of it? If so, how?

In my case, I decided to cut on commute time because it was a big chunk of time that I could use with my family instead. I could use that new routine to prototype what life would feel and look like when I took my sabbatical.

3 – Create a plan in phases with actionable items

In my case, phase one was to find a role closer to me and use the time I would otherwise spend commuting with self-care and my family. Phase two was the execution of communicating the sabbatical and taking it. My actionable items for phase one were:

- Creating a spreadsheet that lists banks and other financial services institutions around my home.

- Spending some time checking for open roles on different banks' career websites.

- Having calls with headhunters to understand what the open role inventory looked like.

- Connecting with my network.

My actionable item for phase two was to ensure I would keep in touch with my network during my sabbatical. Remember, this was a "to be continued" and not a "goodbye."

4 – Create and execute a prototype

Experiment with a prototype version of what the new life could feel and look like. In my case, my prototype was when I started working for the European bank. I had more time for myself and my family, so I had a better idea of what the sabbatical would be like. Friend, remember: You can always pivot the plan when you prototype.

For a long time, I felt like I was excelling more in my role as a Wall Street Vice President than in my role as a mother, which weighed on me. This feeling and my exit strategy made the bidding-farewell process easier. A year after drafting my plan, I bid farewell to Bank 2. I transitioned to the European bank, which was twenty minutes away from my home. I could calmly wake up in the morning, do yoga and meditate, prepare the kids for the day, drop Juliette off in daycare, and still get to the office on time. I have not had that for a long time and missed every second. I liked the prototype; it was working, and I was excited about taking the sabbatical in 2021. Juliette was set to begin kindergarten in September 2021, making it an opportune moment for me to be there alongside her as she embarked on her first school journey in the US. Executing the prototype—testing the plan on a smaller scale to see if spending less time involved with work and more time with my family was what I was after— It was critical for me. Taking the sabbatical was going to be next, due in 2021. Little did I know life was yet to surprise us and force me to press the "reset" button much earlier.

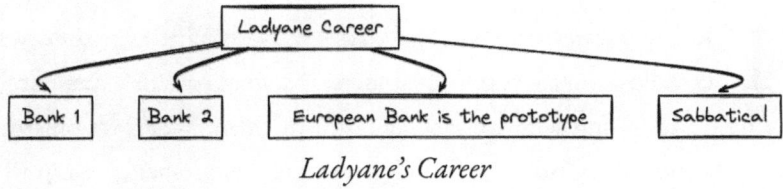

Ladyane's Career

Chapter 10

BIDDING
FAREWELL

*Unpleasant truths bring up big feelings and make
us feel vulnerable. However, where there is vulnerability, there is potential. There is evolving. There is
transformation. And that's beautiful.*

TRANSFORMATION HAPPENS WHEN WE stop. When we pause, we
can allow ourselves to fully understand what specific experiences
bring up to us and who we are as a result of them. When we breathe
steadily, allowing ourselves to be fully present in that moment, we can ask
ourselves, not expecting a straightforward answer: what is my intention?
We do not need to know the answer right away. Transformation is a
process. But when we manifest that intention by asking ourselves, we
can reveal many truths and answers about ourselves and those around
us. They may be unpleasant truths, like the one that goes something
like this: It's emotionally and physically challenging to raise children
when we, women, have demanding and stressful careers. Ultimately,
something needs to give in so there is more space for the other one to

manifest itself. It shouldn't be this way, but this is what society expects of us. Unpleasant truths bring up big feelings and make us feel vulnerable. However, where there is vulnerability, there is potential. There is evolving. There is transformation. And that's beautiful. I know you may have an unpleasant truth about your life that brings up big feelings and makes you feel vulnerable, the beauty of allowing yourself to feel and be this way is that you can turn that into a positive—you can learn. You can evolve. You can transform.

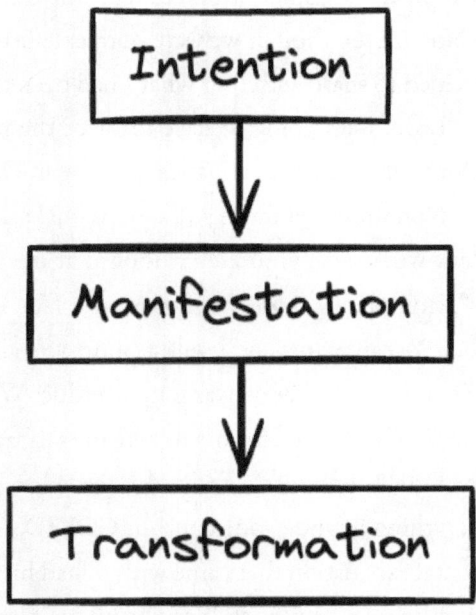

Personal Transformation Path

As I started my new life, a few months short of completing one year in the European bank, life changed once again due to unforeseen circumstances. COVID-19 started. Can you remember a time in our lives when we were more vulnerable than when the entire world went into global lockdown? I cannot. Our parents likely cannot either, nor the generation before them. Nothing compares to the fear and uncertainty of those days. I felt more vulnerable than ever before. The US government declared a national emergency on March 13, 2020, and I worked harder during the following nine months than I ever had in my life.

Meanwhile, I tried to be a good mother, an emotionally available wife, a present daughter, and a supporting sister. It was difficult. I was a high achiever in one role and underperforming in another. It was overwhelming.

But, friend, COVID presented me with the silver lining—COVID was, ultimately, the final push I needed to press the "emotional reset" button. One day in the summer, after we had put the kids in bed, I sat down with Noah. Even though we were both exhausted and needed quiet time, I decided to share with him what I had been thinking about for a few days: "Love, I am going to have to pivot the plan. I think it would be best for us if I took the sabbatical starting in December. This way, you can focus on the career move you want to make, and I can focus on us. This is not working anymore." He looked at me with a relieved gaze and said, "I completely understand how you feel. I think it's the right thing to do. We can manage it. I will support you all the way." We both hugged. We knew the change was long overdue. We had planned for it. We had originally planned for me to take my sabbatical sometime in the summer of 2021, however, I realized I needed to pivot the plan because not everything is under our control. COVID, along with the physical and mental exhaustion that came with it, had hit me. Long and stressful working hours and two children at home with no childcare during COVID made me reach my limit. I needed a less hectic pace and the ability to properly and intentionally care for my children, family, and myself.

Not Sticking Around To Find Out

Accepting and recognizing variables on your path to (re)designing your best life is critical to ensuring your plan succeeds.

During the pandemic, I struggled to navigate life under sudden lockdowns while balancing my career, raising two young children, and fulfilling my roles as a wife, daughter, sister, and friend. I found myself awake on endless nights, gasping for air. For the first time since a stressful summer internship interview, I experienced a panic attack. I found comfort in my inner voice, saying to myself: *Find a safe mental place, Ladyane. Breathe. Do nothing. Stay steady, strong, and vigilant. Avoid dwelling on 'What ifs' and the uncertainty.*

On one hand, many variables were beyond my control. On the other hand, everything I thought I could manage, like motherhood, seemed to be slipping away. Childcare services were closed, plans had to be changed, and my Brazilian relatives were falling ill due to COVID. I was overwhelmed by the uncertainty and fear about whether my children would ever have a normal life without masks. My career, which I had planned to put on hold only in the summer of 2021, had unexpectedly become a priority much earlier—I saw myself working long hours, nonstop. That summer night, I found myself gasping for air, questioning what had just happened and why I was feeling afraid again.

Breathe, Ladyane.

Breathe, Ladyane. Steady.

Breathe, Ladyane. Strong.

Breathe, Ladyane. Vigilant.

Plan, Ladyane. Manifest, Ladyane.

Friend, let me provide some context about my Wall Street career. I specialized in risk management, focusing on compliance and regulatory and operational risks. My role involved overseeing and leading initiatives based on the risk frameworks and profiles of the banks where I worked.

When the World Health Organization (WHO) declared a global pandemic, it presented unprecedented challenges for financial institutions. I had to rapidly shift my focus from my usual responsibilities to develop and lead initiatives to create new policies, procedures, and processes to manage and mitigate the pandemic's impact on the bank and its customers.

From a risk management perspective, my job was to reassess the bank's operational risk appetite and exposure in light of the pandemic-induced uncertainties while trying to keep business operations running smoothly. I spearheaded operational resilience efforts, ensuring that the organization could maintain its daily functions even if staff were absent or technology failed.

The situation was particularly challenging during the pandemic as staff members either fell ill or had family members in the hospital. Three to four months after March 2020, I felt like gasping for air again while riding an enormous wave. People lost jobs, businesses closed, rents went unpaid, and loans defaulted. Despite the intense pressure and spotlight at work, I also had to be present for my children at home. To this day, I am amazed at how I accomplished so much during those stressful and uncertain times.

That summer night, after I had caught up with my feelings, I got up from bed. I sat down in my office located in the quiet corner of my basement and calmly drafted a coverage proposal for my role at the bank; my rationale was that I needed to have a plan in case my manager was going to be receptive to my ask. The next day, I put a fifteen-minute call on my manager's calendar, and the conversation went something like this:

Ladyane: "I need to slow down."

Manager: "It has been too much, right?"

Ladyane: "Yes. It has been too much, and it's taking a toll on me. I want to slow down."

Manager: "I see. I understand. How much of you can you give us?"

Ladyane: "I can distribute the work between X, Y, and Z. I will train X to cover the monthly regulatory meetings. This way, we can gradually reduce my hours from what I do today to about thirty to twenty hours. We can do it in phases. I will send you the plan."

Manager: "That sounds great. Send me the details, and let's make it happen. Take whatever you need to recharge. We can't afford to lose you."

A month or so went by, and the reality was different from what I had hoped and planned for. I sometimes needed to do the same amount of work but in fewer hours. So, I quickly recognized and accepted that I needed to pivot my plan. You see, friend, do you remember the plan for living your best life? The most significant piece to this plan is to accept that some things are out of your control and recognize when it's time to pivot your plan. Identifying the main driver for pivoting the plan is essential, too. Accepting and recognizing variables on your path to (re)designing your best life is critical to ensuring your plan succeeds. No one else can do it for you; no one else has the ability and the same intention you do for (re)designing your best life. No one can identify and accept certain variables that could, ultimately, make you pivot your plan. Only you can—you are in charge, and only you can pivot the plan and the path forward. Always look ahead, beyond that wave.

A few months later, despite reducing my hours, I realized I was still unhappy and not finding the relief I needed. So, I decided to move up my sabbatical and submitted my resignation. I was determined to avoid the long-term effects of the stressful lifestyle I was leading—I didn't want to wait and see how it might impact me in the future. My plan was already in place; I needed to acknowledge my emotional and physical limits. Recognizing that I had reached my limit wasn't a sign of weakness or quitting, it was an understanding of what I needed and what I didn't want. It meant I had a clearer sense of myself, which is a significant aspect of personal growth.

When I resigned, my manager was shocked. He hadn't anticipated it because I had always presented a façade of handling everything well, saying, "It's all crazy. It's a lot. But I am handling it." I was projecting an image of control to uphold the belief that "perception is reality." In truth, I was masking the stress I was experiencing for a purpose that no longer resonated with me. The purpose had changed, and I needed to act on it.

In hindsight, I realized that my manager offered me flexibility and tried to find a solution for me to stay so I could have time to breathe and recharge. Over the next two business days, we discussed various options for me to stay, but none met my needs or tempted me to remain. I realized I needed a break from the environment hindering my ability to embrace my next purpose—being an emotionally present and intentional mother.

During the next few days after I announced my resignation, coworkers kept reaching out, trying to understand if this was a "Ladyane will be right back" or "I will see you when I see you" type of resignation. I honestly did not know which one I was going with; I wanted to enjoy being a mother. I told everyone that I needed and wanted to be with my children. I told everyone I craved moments I had already missed with them and would have to play catch up—first words, discoveries, giggles due to silly moments, tantrums that needed my attention, and challenges that required hand-holding and emotional coaching.

You see, I was exhausted from feeling like I was barely getting by. I was intense, intentional, and a high achiever. I wanted to be a high achiever in my most important role—being a mother to my children in a meaningful and purposeful way. I didn't want to just go through the motions of motherhood—feeding, bathing, putting them to bed, and repeating. I wanted to engage in the intentional, loving labor of being a present and involved mother.

I was ready to move beyond the routine tasks and pursue this new purpose. Juliette was four years old, and Gabriel was two, and I deeply yearned for time with them. This intentional and emotionally present motherly presence was something I did not have much of while growing up due to the challenges my mother faced in raising me and my siblings after my father passed. There I was again, trying to break another generational cycle. Despite the immense challenges, my mother raised us with unwavering dignity and integrity, embodying an extraordinary commitment to our well-being. I will always be profoundly grateful for her remarkable ability to adapt and reinvent herself.

During my last call with my manager, we bid farewell and agreed to be in touch. We decided this was a to-be-continued farewell rather than an ultimate and final goodbye. This mindset helped me to be less afraid of the change—I liked knowing the doors were open should I decide to return. I enjoyed having this notion of job security. I will always be thankful for the professional relationships I built in all the banks I worked at. My former managers and I still keep in touch and get together when possible. We chat about life, the market, work, and my ability to return and start where I paused. I joke and say, "If and when I come back, you'll meet a brand-new Ladyane—one who's mastered the art of balancing priorities and has finally figured out where the 'off' switch is!"

I'm uncertain whether I'll ever return to Wall Street. From what I hear, the landscape has shifted somewhat due to COVID, with banks adopting a new focus on work-life balance. Yet, some work colleagues tell me this remains largely aspirational rather than actualized. While Wall Street remains a powerful platform for career advancement and personal achievement, I doubt that the typical investment bank can genuinely support the work–life balance that women of my generation deeply desire. I hope I'm mistaken, and that genuine change is underway. I wish the industry would place a stronger emphasis on women's mental health and acknowledge the immense mental load we carry. We should be empowered to make a difference in the industry without sacrificing the many roles and identities we embrace. These roles are valuable and essential; we shouldn't have to diminish or conceal them to succeed. Instead, we should be encouraged to embrace and integrate them fully.

See the Path Forward, Beyond the Emotional Wave

Being able to envision a path forward while riding immense emotional waves is both liberating and transformative.

Friend, faced with instability and hardship from a young age, I learned to envision a path beyond pain, adversity, and uncertainty. Even when I couldn't always see it clearly, I developed a way to keep moving forward. I manifested the life I wanted by speaking to myself when I needed it most, picturing a future where I had overcome the challenges before me. Visualizing life after overcoming obstacles became a crucial part of the process. Whenever I felt afraid or overwhelmed, I imagined what life could be like once I conquered those hurdles. Over time, I created a mantra to guide me through tough times, complemented by breathing techniques and coping strategies to navigate the emotional waves that life brings.

Despite years of deep emotional grief from losing my father at a young age, I learned to navigate the turbulent waves of my emotions. I discovered how to cultivate inner stability, finding freedom and transformation in the process. Being able to envision a path forward while riding immense emotional waves is both liberating and transformative. It allows you to repurpose pain and life's challenges towards a greater purpose: the purpose of personal transformation.

Self-awareness, intention, manifestation, and action empower us to ride that enormous emotional wave and see the path forward as if almost at our fingertips. My path forward was right before my eyes. In the days following my last day at work, I planned and executed the path forward—the path I manifested in the following days after my resignation. I was emotionally and intentionally available for my children and myself. My feelings were crystal clear. It was time for a new beginning. It was time to deliberately and intentionally execute my new purpose, the one of being the heart and soul of my people.

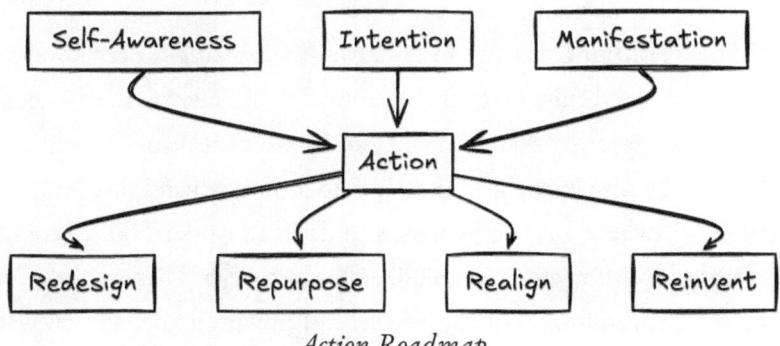

Action Roadmap

A few months after my resignation, I had a quick call with my former manager. We exchanged thoughts on the market, and he asked if I planned to return to work. I told him about my life then and how much I enjoyed it. We talked about how the kids grew up fast and how much I enjoyed being with them. I told him if I were to return, I wanted to work from home a few days a week with no traveling so that I could easily transition to supporting the children when I was home. He agreed and said he would have a role for me in the first quarter of 2022 and that we should keep talking because he would love to bring me back for that particular role. Before we hung up, we agreed we would catch up every two months. After we hung up, I called Noah and told him about the role details and the timing; I had mixed feelings about it.

Noah: "You must be feeling good knowing they are open to having you back, right?"

Ladyane: "Yes, for sure. This means a lot to me."

Noah: "It's been less than six months since you stopped. You do not need to rush to commit to this. We are good. Are you sure you want to return so soon?

Ladyane: "No. I am not sure. I do not think I am in a good place to decide this right now. But it makes me feel good to know that my hard work still pays off and makes me relevant. We will catch up again in two months. I will think about that again as I hear more about the role."

Noah: "I think your plan is a good plan."

I knew returning to work in 2022 was premature—I needed more time to reset and fully grasp the meaning of that mental and physical break. I was savoring that "time off" and wasn't yet ready to return; I wanted to be sure I felt a genuine desire to return, which I didn't at the time. And, believe me, I knew what that desire to work felt like; I could remember how that ambition felt like back in college. That ambition of launching a promising Wall Street career and growing in the industry was dormant—it no longer existed. Career ambition and motivation were replaced by a feeling that a big change would come. I felt something significant was on the horizon, but I couldn't pinpoint it. It was as if I needed a clear sign or guidance to show me the way forward. I longed for something or someone to lead me, to say, *"Here, Ladyane. This is your new path. This is your evolved self. This is how life will feel from now on."* I was deeply invested in myself and my family, and I wasn't ready to let go of that feeling.

Stay-At-Home Mom – The Role of Raising My Children

We are designed to make significant decisions and drive meaningful change.

Transitioning from a high-achieving and fast-paced Wall Street career into a physically and emotionally demanding role of being an emotionally and intentionally present mother was the hardest thing I have ever done. It took me some time to be more graceful with myself. It took me time to learn how to better understand my children. It took me time to create a new rhythm for our routine. It took me and Noah some time to (re)design the new family dynamic. More importantly, it took me time to find myself in this new role; I needed to (re)align myself with the new daily tasks, the routine, and each child's needs.

When I meet people for the first time, and they ask what I do, I say, "Today, I raise my children."

Why don't I label myself a stay-at-home mom? I honestly believe that the term does nothing for me. Instead, it carries a load of societal stereotypes that undermine who I truly am and the person I've become. This label often prevents others from seeing beyond the surface—obscuring my journey, story, and growth. And let me tell you, there is immense power in our stories.

The label "stay-at-home mom" is a social construct that overlooks the profound personal growth we experience and our vital role in shaping our children into good human beings. It fails to acknowledge the challenges I faced before and after becoming a mother while also managing a demanding career on Wall Street. The true focus here is that a mother's journey is unique, and the value of raising our children extends far beyond any superficial measure of emotional effort or financial dependence. Each family's dynamics and financial paths are personal choices and shouldn't be judged or labeled. What truly matters is recognizing the genuine effort women put into raising their children. We are designed to make significant decisions and drive meaningful change.

Some may think this label suggests I spend my days preparing snacks, scheduling playdates, and shuttling kids to activities. Yes, I do these tasks, but they don't capture the whole picture. In reality, here is what I do: I perform the mentally challenging, ever-demanding, equally rewarding labor of love. I do not pretend I know it all, but I embrace the deeply fulfilling labor of raising my children.

Society's views on stay-at-home moms are divided. Some admire my commitment to raising my children, while others dismiss my worth, believing my contribution should be rooted in traditional employment. Four years ago, when I paused my career, I shared this latter view—I struggled with the idea of not contributing financially to my family. At the time, I didn't realize that I had already achieved financial stability through my hard work, breaking the cycle of fearing instability.

I also underestimated that the labor of love requires profound self-awareness. To mother my children intentionally and be emotionally present, I had to confront my faults, doubts, and misconceptions and build a new belief system that I didn't have growing up. This personal growth, in itself, has become my reward.

If the Ladyane of four years ago could see the lessons learned and the healing experienced from pausing her career to dedicate herself to intentional mothering, she might have embraced the decision with more grace and less self-criticism. She would have thought: *This journey will bring healing, nurturing, and challenges. It won't be easy, but it will be magical.*

As time passed and our family adjusted to the new routine of my constant presence, Noah and I began to wonder if it was the right moment to grow our family. We were uncertain. On one hand, I grappled with the lingering impacts of COVID—losing relatives to the virus in unexpected ways, such as through overwhelmed hospitals or lack of vaccines, left me struggling to cope with their loss and the inability to say goodbye properly. On the other hand, expanding our family had always been part of our plan. I've always envisioned a home filled with children and the joyful sounds of their laughter. To me, the best soundtrack is to listen to my children's laughs and giggles.

Noah and I discussed whether we should wait and see how the post-COVID world would unfold. We were gradually adjusting to socializing again and adapting to a new "normal." We felt like we were getting a handle on what life would look like after COVID, and things seemed to be falling back into place. However, after about two months, I found myself making unexpected changes to our plans. It became clear that the significant change I had been anticipating was actually taking place.

The Wishful Surprise—The Element of Not Being in Control

Have you ever sensed that something significant is about to change, but you can't quite tell what it is? That's how I felt months before becoming pregnant with our baby girl. Looking back, I believe that by talking and planning so much about having a third child, Noah and I unintentionally brought about the greatest joy for our family—a joyful, giggly, and energetic baby girl. Our little baby girl, Sarah, arrived in March 2022, a true blessing for us.

Nine months before March 2022, I could barely believe those pregnancy tests. It was a Saturday morning, and I was dealing with a hangover from a night of wine at our friends' house while the kids ran wild. I always despised the day after drinking—thirsty and headachy. I remember thinking, *That's it! I'm done with drinking. My New Year's resolution is set—I'm quitting for good! My body is clearly sending me a message.* It took me three years to actually follow through, but hey, better late than never, right?

Back to that fateful Saturday morning—my period was a few days late, but I barely noticed. Despite the hangover and my desperate need to drink a lake of water, I decided to take a pregnancy test. There I was, peeing on the stick while my head throbbed, and I mentally resolved to quit drinking, starting that very day. *I'll just get this over with*, I thought, *the stick will say 'Not pregnant,' and then I can get my period and get on with life.*

I brushed my teeth and washed my face, giving that test ample time to confirm my suspicions so I could move on. After five minutes of pampering my hangover, I grabbed the stick, expecting the usual *Not pregnant* result. But when I saw *Pregnant* on the test, I froze. I blinked, thinking my blurry vision was a side effect of my hangover.

I rushed to get another test, chugged more water, and waited an hour to pee again. *Pregnant* showed up once more. Shocked and thrilled, I burst into tears, ran out of the bathroom, and caught Noah's eye. I waved him over without saying a word, and he sprinted to the bathroom.

Still crying, I pointed at the tests and said, "Look at this!" Noah took one glance, his eyes brimming with tears, and simply asked, "Are you serious?" We hugged, shaking and crying, overwhelmed by the surprise. It was the most memorable moment because we had both longed for our baby girl and let life take its course, letting go of the steering wheel and allowing ourselves to be guided. We held each other close, drying our tears, and said, "I love you so much," in the most heartfelt embrace.

Noah and I had longed for that Saturday morning with all our hearts. We were eager to expand our family, but fear held us back. The year leading up to that Saturday was tumultuous—juggling relentless work schedules while navigating a pandemic with two young children left us feeling lost. There were no guides for living through such unprecedented times.

Sarah is a symbol of renewal, marking a transformation in our lives that would never return to what it once was. Sarah reshaped everything. Gabriel was no longer the youngest; Juliette became a big sister with newfound dedication, patience, and love. Noah embraced the pregnancy and our evolving family dynamic as though he was always meant to be a father of three. And I felt ready and profoundly blessed.

Once again, I embraced my role with the same enthusiasm and optimism as that young Ladyane, who had just arrived in the US, ready to start anew. Life had begun again, a fresh chapter full of hope, transformation, and purpose.

Personal Transformation Is Inevitable

Evolving doesn't close doors—it opens new ones through the continuous growth and learning we pursue.

Two months had passed since I last spoke with my former manager, so it was time for another catch-up call. I was nervous about sharing the news of my pregnancy. I feared that the pregnancy might close doors for me, feeling like I was saying goodbye rather than just "see you later." A few minutes before the call, I sat down to journal, hoping to clarify my feelings and prepare for what was about to happen. Here's what I wrote:

Steady.

Strong.

Vigilant.

There is more learning. There is more healing. There is more living. There is more being.

There, friend: *There is more being.*

While focusing on my children and personal growth at home, I discovered that transforming life's adversities into opportunities for personal development requires three essential pillars: self-awareness, continuous learning (embracing mistakes as part of the learning process), and recognizing our achievements. As I journaled before my call with my former manager, I realized I had reached a significant milestone in my 'stay-at-home mom' journey. I was clear about my emotions and knew what to say and how to describe them, thanks to lessons learned from past mistakes in setting personal boundaries at work.

Here I was, three months pregnant with my third child, six months into a sabbatical, preparing for a call to discuss my return to work. I recognized that I had broken free from old patterns and could now enjoy my growing family without the pressure to rush back to my career. Far from closing a door, I had opened several doors to exciting new possibilities for my life. This realization was beyond what my younger self could have imagined. My journal entry concluded with this:

I do not need to return right now. I know this is what life is meant to be for now—this is me now, and it is part of my process. I can stop running from the rock chasing me. I am here to heal. I am here to raise my children during the most critical years—to establish a strong foundation for them to be naturally resilient and emotionally intelligent individuals.

Friend, a Hebrew term called *Mitzvah* encompasses several meaningful concepts in Jewish tradition. In essence, a mitzvah is an act of kindness or a good deed performed with a deep sense of purpose or duty. At that moment, I couldn't think of a more important duty than fulfilling my lifelong desire to raise my children. I called my manager, shared the news of my pregnancy, and thanked him for considering me. I explained that I wanted to stay home for an extended period to be fully present during my baby girl's first year and transition smoothly into life with three children.

He was excited about the news and encouraged me to keep in touch, expressing his confidence that I would return one day. We still catch up from time to time. This experience taught me that evolving doesn't close doors—it opens new ones through the continuous growth and learning we pursue. Achieving this mindset requires focusing on self-awareness, embracing lifelong learning, and recognizing our achievements and challenges.

Friend, I've learned that job titles are fleeting, but the personal transformation you undergo and the impact it has on your life and those around you are what truly endure. That impact becomes your legacy. While some may try to confine you with labels or judge your changes, others will celebrate your growth and the positive effects you've made. I always try to stick beside those who celebrate my narrative and understand I am who I am because of what I have gone through.

The lesson I strive to impart to my children is that who I am and who I have become is shaped by my life's journey—by the adversities, harsh truths, challenges, and accomplishments. I am committed to staying true to my story and honest with my narrative. I refuse to downplay my struggles and fears; instead, I embrace them and navigate them with purpose and resilience.

From my childhood, I experienced the deepest form of grief—losing a parent. As I entered adulthood, I faced life's challenges head-on, driven by fear rather than choice. It took me time to realize that I didn't have to confront adversity out of fear and that it's possible to find a path forward even amidst overwhelming challenges.

Despite the years it took me to process my grief over my father's passing, I have come to deeply admire the strength of the woman who raised me—my mother. Her life is a powerful story of adaptability, resilience, and transformation. From her childhood in northeastern Brazil, without electricity to her move to a larger city in search of better opportunities, through her struggle in an abusive marriage, and her reinvention at thirty-five as a widow with three children to raise, she has faced and overcome immense challenges. At fifty-seven, she began a new chapter in a foreign country, embracing a new culture and overcoming language barriers. Her journey is a remarkable example of the power of transformation.

What I'm illustrating here, friend, is that change is a natural part of life. We are meant to evolve and transform, continuously breaking unhealthy cycles and striving to live our best lives. Some of us may get caught up in the path of doubt—unclear about the purpose while questioning the process of change—undermining all the possibilities that could once become reality. Others embrace this path, make a plan, and act on it. Both paths are part of the personal growth journey and should be recognized, accepted, and celebrated. One is not better than the other. They simply show different ways to ride the emotional wave—to deal with the change.

I discovered the power of envisioning a path forward, regardless of the circumstances. I manifested the moments I longed for, persevering through challenges and learning to navigate emotional highs and lows. In the corporate world, I mastered creating a safety zone with a clear purpose. I pivoted once again when I felt fulfilled and ready for a new chapter.

I realized that true emotional stability comes from within, not from job titles or impressive paychecks. I learned to (re)design, (re)purpose, and (re)invent my life for something greater, ultimately (re)aligning my trajectory. Was I apprehensive about putting my high-achieving career on indefinite hold? Absolutely. But I refused to let fear take control. Instead, I let fear accompany me on the emotional journey without allowing it to dictate how I ride the waves of change.

How about you? Can you rewrite your personal speech? Can you rewrite your context? Your narrative? Here's how today's Ladyane would express her transformation if she were to give a speech today:

"Good evening, ladies and gentlemen,

I was born in a very small town in Brazil, Cuiabá, close to one of the biggest swamps in the world, Pantanal. In fact, the swamp is actually bigger than the town. Back then, most of the streets had no pavement, and houses were very modest, with brick walls and no paint. This is where I come from, and I want to share my story of personal growth with you, driven by self-awareness, continuous learning, and acknowledgment of my failures and successes.

We are not defined solely by our virtues. Our life experiences—both the highs and the lows—shape us into who we become at various stages in our lives. For much of my young adulthood, I wrestled with the fear of reliving the financial instability and uncertainties I had left behind in Brazil. This fear drove me to achieve success on Wall Street, where I found financial stability and built my safety zone. But as life often does, it brought new experiences that transformed me.

Becoming a mother was a profound change. Today, I am the mother of three incredible children. With each child, a new version of me was born—steadier, stronger, and more vigilant. I pushed myself to my emotional and physical limits and decided to pause my career to focus on the labor of love: connecting deeply and intentionally with my children. Growing up, I missed out on this connection, having lost my father when I was just seven. My role model, my mother, struggled to make ends meet. My purpose became breaking that cycle of struggle and providing my children with emotional stability.

In dedicating myself to this new role, I discovered not just how to nurture my children but also how to grow and heal personally. This journey of transformation led me to an unexpected crossroads. A conversation with a friend sparked a question that changed everything: 'Why don't you write a book about your journey? There's so much you can share.'

And so, here it is—my journey, my lessons, and my narrative. Now, I turn the question to you: Are you ready to change your own narrative? Are you ready to take control of your emotions, embrace your desires, accept your fears, and (re)align your priorities? Are you prepared to (re)design your life, (re)purpose your roles and labels, and (re)invent yourself? Are you ready to ride the wave of change and rewrite your personal speech?

I chose to (re)align my priorities, (re)design my life, (re)purpose my roles, and (re)invent myself as a wife, a Jewish woman, a mother, and a former Wall Street executive. I've crafted a new version of Ladyane—one who knows how to set boundaries, practice self-awareness, balance different roles and priorities, and ride emotional waves in life.

Now, it's your turn. The power to transform your life is in your hands. Embrace it."

GRATITUDE

WRITING THIS BOOK HAS been a deeply personal and transformative journey, one that would not have been possible without the support of many incredible people in my life. I am forever grateful for the village that has surrounded me with love, encouragement, and wisdom throughout this process.

To my family—my wonderful husband and our beautiful children—thank you for your boundless patience, love, and understanding. Your unwavering belief in me gave me the strength to pursue this dream, even on the toughest days. To my mother and sister, your love and support throughout my life have been the foundation upon which I've built this journey. Thank you for believing in me every step of the way.

To my writing mentor, Larissa Rinaldi, your guidance has been invaluable. Your insightful feedback, patience, and encouragement have shaped this book in ways I couldn't have imagined. I am deeply thankful for the wisdom you imparted, the conversations we shared, and for pushing me to dig deeper into my narrative.

To my dearest friends and early readers, thank you for your thoughtful feedback and for embracing this project with such enthusiasm. You helped me refine my voice and gave me the confidence to share this story with the world.

A special thank you to the incredible community of women and mentors who have been my source of strength and inspiration. You have helped me see the power of my voice and reminded me of the importance of lifting each other up.

Finally, to all the women who will pick up this book—I wrote it for you. My hope is that it inspires you to embrace change, overcome life's challenges, and discover the strength that lies within you. Thank you for being part of this journey.

With gratitude and love,

Ladyane

STAY CONNECTED

THANK YOU FOR JOINING me on this journey through *The Waves We Ride.* The stories and lessons shared in these pages are only the beginning, and I would love to continue the conversation with you. Whether you're seeking guidance, inspiration, or simply looking to connect with like-minded women, there are several ways we can stay in touch:

- **Website:** Visit for updates on future projects, workshops, and new content aimed at helping you embrace change and create the life you want. Here, you'll find resources, blog posts, and tools that expand on the themes of this book.

- **Social Media:** Follow me on Instagram at , where I share daily tips, inspiration, and behind-the-scenes glimpses into my life as an entrepreneur, mother, and advocate for women's empowerment. Let's connect and build a community that uplifts and supports one another.

- **Newsletter:** Subscribe to my newsletter for exclusive content, updates on my upcoming workshops and events, and deeper insights into how to build your *Supporting Village.* I'm excited to share more tools to help you create meaningful change and thrive in all areas of your life.

- **Workshops & Events:** I offer workshops, including the *Supporting Village Vision Board*, designed to help you surround yourself with people who uplift, support, and inspire you. Stay tuned for announcements on upcoming events where we can connect, learn, and grow together.

Let's continue riding the waves of life, embracing each challenge with strength and grace. I look forward to hearing your stories, witnessing your growth, and supporting you as you create your own path.

With gratitude,

Ladyane

Stay in Touch!

www.ingramcontent.com/pod-product-compliance
Lightning Source LLC
Chambersburg PA
CBHW020823150626
46554CB00017B/1881